This Textbook is useful for Savitribai Phule Pune University and other Universities of Maharashtra as well as Competitive Exams.

BUSINESS ADMINISTRATION

(Corporate Social Responsibility)

(Course Code : CS569MJ)

M.Com. - I (Sem. - II)

As per New Education Policy (2020)

Dr. Yashodhan Mithare
(M.Com., Ph.D.)
Haribhai V. Desai College of Commerce, Arts and Science, Pune.

Dr. M. G. Mulla
(M.Com., M.M.S., M.Phil., P.G.D.I.B. D.T.L. DLL & LW G.D.C&A., Ph.D.)
MCE Society Abeda Inamdar Senior College of Arts, Science and Commerce, Pune.

Dr. Kavita Vaswani
(M.Com., M.Phil., SET., Ph.D.)
Haribhai V. Desai College of Commerce, Arts and Science, Pune.

Dr. Anand Kore
(M.Com., M.Phil., SET., Ph.D.)
Haribhai V. Desai College of Commerce, Arts and Science, Pune.

2024

Price: 80/-

SUCCESS PUBLICATIONS

Published by
Dr. Rajesh M. Patne
Success Publications
Radha Krishna Apartment, 535, Shaniwar Peth,
Appa Balwant Chowk, Opp. Prabhat Talkies, Pune - 411 030.
Mobile: 9325315464, 8390848833

Edition
2024

Edited By
Mr. Valmik Gaikwad

Typesetting, Layout
Mr. Valmik Gaikwad

Cover Designing
Miss. Varsha Lokhande

ISBN NO. – 978-81-19939-58-9

Preface

It is a matter of great pleasure for us to present this book to our esteemed readers. This book has been designed as standard text on '(Business Administration (Corporate Social Responsibility))' for M.Com. (Sem. - II).

This book comprehensively covers thc cntirc syllabus of M.Com. 'Corporate Social Responsibility ' Course of Savitribai Phule Pune University effective from 2023 onwards. It has been written to meet the requirements of students of M.Com. Some of the special features of the book are as follows:

1. *Full coverage of the revised syllabus of M.Com.*
2. *Chapter outline at the beginning of each chapter to give a bird's eye view of the topics covered in the chapter.*
3. *Point wise explanation of each topic in the chapter.*
4. *Topics are logically arranged in numbered paragraphs exactly according to the modified syllabus.*
5. *Proposed questions at the end of each chapter.*
6. *Extensive use of diagrams, tables and various forms to give visual view of key concepts and techniques.*
7. *Conversational, lucid and simple language.*

Every effort has been made to provide the readers with most up-to-date and authentic material on the subject.

We are very grateful to our publisher Mrs. and Mr. Rajesh Patne who have rendered all possible assistance in bringing out this book. We wish to acknowledge our deep gratitude to staff who have assisted and helped us in preparing this book. We will consider our efforts amply rewarded in case the book proves useful to the students and teachers of the subject.

Suggestions of readers are welcome and shall be acknowledged with gratitude.

With best wishes.

By Authors

Syllabus

M.Com. - I (Sem. - II) (Business Administration)
Corporate Social Responsibility (Course Code: CS569MJ)

Unit	Topic	Lectures
1	**FUNDAMENTAL CONCEPTS OF CORPORATE SOCIAL RESPONSIBILITY** **1.1** Introduction to CSR: Concept, definition, scope **1.2** Evolution of CSR. The evolving role of stakeholders **1.3** CSR towards stakeholders **1.4** CSR policy and governance **1.5** Theories & Models of CSR	15
2	**STAKEHOLDERS MANAGEMENT AND ENGAGEMENT** **2.1** Introducing a systems-based approach to developing CSR **2.2** Assessing the current state of a company's CSR activities **2.3** Implementing CSR programmes **2.4** Monitoring and measuring the impact of CSR programs **2.5** Moral and economic arguments for CSR	15

INDEX

M.Com. - I (Sem. - II) (Business Administration)
Corporate Social Responsibility (Course Code: CS569MJ)

UNIT 1

Fundamental Concept of Corporate Social Responsibility

Introduction:

Corporate social responsibility (CSR) is a multifaceted and evolving concept that encapsulates a wide array of fundamental principles and practices aimed at fostering ethical, sustainable, and socially responsible behavior within the corporate sphere. At its core, CSR embodies the idea that businesses have a moral and ethical obligation to go beyond mere profit maximization and consider the broader impact of their actions on society, the environment, and stakeholders. Key fundamental concepts of CSR include ethical business conduct, which emphasizes honesty, integrity, and transparency in all corporate dealings, as well as responsible environmental stewardship, involving initiatives to reduce ecological footprints, minimize resource consumption, and mitigate climate change. Furthermore, CSR entails a commitment to the well-being of employees, encompassing fair labor practices, diversity and inclusion, safe working conditions, and employee development. Additionally, CSR extends to philanthropy and community engagement, where companies contribute to societal welfare through charitable giving, volunteerism, and community partnerships. Moreover, CSR calls for responsible supply chain management, ensuring that business operations do not exploit vulnerable populations or compromise human rights. Beyond these aspects, CSR also involves governance and accountability, promoting ethical leadership, effective governance structures, and transparent reporting mechanisms to maintain public trust. Ultimately, CSR is a dynamic and evolving concept that continues to evolve with changing societal expectations and environmental challenges, prompting businesses to adapt and integrate these fundamental principles into their core strategies to create a more sustainable and equitable future for all.

1.1 Introduction to CSR:

Corporate Social Responsibility (CSR) is a vital framework that has gained increasing prominence in the global business landscape. It represents a commitment by organizations to go beyond profit generation and actively consider their impact on society, the environment, and stakeholders. CSR encompasses a wide range of ethical and sustainable practices, including responsible business conduct, environmental sustainability, employee well-being, community engagement, ethical supply chain management, and transparent governance. In an era characterized by growing social and environmental challenges, CSR serves as a guiding principle for businesses to align their operations with broader societal goals, foster trust among stakeholders, and contribute to a more equitable and sustainable world. This introduction sets the stage for exploring the multifaceted dimensions of CSR and its significance in contemporary business practices.

1.1.1 Meaning:

Corporate Social Responsibility (CSR) is a strategic approach that embodies a company's commitment to conducting its business in an ethical, sustainable, and socially responsible manner. It involves the voluntary integration of environmental, social, and governance considerations into a company's operations and decision-making processes. CSR encompasses a wide range of initiatives, including ethical business practices, environmental stewardship, support for communities and employees, responsible supply chain management, and transparent corporate governance. By embracing CSR, organizations aim to not only generate profits but also contribute positively to society, minimize their environmental footprint, and enhance their relationships with stakeholders, all while upholding ethical values and principles.

1.1.2 Definitions:

Following are the definitions of the CSR:

1) **Archie B. Carroll:**

   "The social responsibility of business encompasses the economic, legal, ethical, and discretionary expectations that society has of organizations at a given point in time."

2) **Milton Friedman:**

   "The social responsibility of business is to increase its profits." He believed that businesses should primarily focus on generating profits within the bounds of the law and without deception or fraud.

3) **Carroll and Shabana:**

   "The social responsibility of business the social obligation of business that encompasses the economic, legal, ethical, and philanthropic expectations that society has of organizations at a given point in time."

4) **Philip Kotler and Nancy Lee:**

"The social responsibility of business a commitment to improve community well-being through discretionary business practices and contributions of corporate resources."

1.1.3 Scope of CSR:

Corporate Social Responsibility (CSR) is a concept that has gained significant prominence in the business world over the past few decades. It refers to a company's ethical and philanthropic responsibilities toward society and the environment beyond its core business operations. CSR encompasses a wide range of activities and initiatives aimed at contributing positively to society.

1) **Historical Evolution of CSR:**

To understand the scope of CSR, it's essential to trace its historical evolution. CSR has evolved from a purely profit-centric approach to a more comprehensive concept encompassing environmental, social, and ethical considerations. Early business practices focused solely on profit maximization, but societal expectations have shifted over time, leading to the development of CSR as we know it today.

2) **Legislation and Regulation:**

Many countries have implemented legislation and regulations that mandate or encourage CSR activities. This includes laws related to environmental protection, labor practices, and corporate governance. Understanding these legal requirements is a fundamental aspect of the CSR scope.

3) **Stakeholder Engagement:**

One of the core principles of CSR is engaging with stakeholders. Companies need to identify and interact with their various stakeholders, including customers, employees, investors, communities, and non-governmental organizations (NGOs). The scope of CSR includes strategies for effectively managing these relationships to address stakeholders' concerns and expectations.

4) **Environmental Sustainability:**

A crucial aspect of CSR is the environmental dimension. Companies are increasingly recognizing their responsibility to minimize their environmental footprint. This includes efforts to reduce carbon emissions, conserve resources, and adopt sustainable practices throughout their supply chains.

5) **Social Responsibility:**

CSR extends to social responsibility, encompassing initiatives that benefit communities and society at large. This includes supporting education, healthcare, poverty alleviation, and social justice causes. The scope of CSR involves identifying the most pressing social issues and aligning corporate resources to address them.

6) Ethical Business Practices:

Ethical considerations play a significant role in CSR. Companies are expected to adhere to ethical business practices, including fair treatment of employees, ethical sourcing of materials, and transparency in financial reporting. The scope of CSR encompasses implementing ethical guidelines and codes of conduct.

7) Philanthropy and Charitable Giving:

Many corporations engage in philanthropic activities as part of their CSR efforts. This can involve donating to charitable organizations, supporting disaster relief efforts, or sponsoring cultural and educational events. The scope of CSR includes defining the extent of such philanthropic endeavors.

8) Employee Well-being and Development:

CSR extends to the well-being and development of employees. This includes providing a safe working environment, offering training and development opportunities, and promoting diversity and inclusion within the workforce. The scope of CSR covers initiatives aimed at enhancing the overall quality of the workplace.

9) Supply Chain Responsibility:

Companies are increasingly held responsible for the actions of their suppliers and partners. CSR involves evaluating and improving the ethical and environmental practices of suppliers, ensuring fair labor conditions, and minimizing risks associated with the supply chain.

10) Community Engagement:

Engaging with local communities is a vital component of CSR. Companies may support community development projects, participate in community-based initiatives, and foster positive relationships with the areas in which they operate. The scope of CSR involves identifying community needs and collaborating on solutions.

11) Measuring Impact and Reporting:

To assess the effectiveness of CSR initiatives, it's crucial to measure their impact. Companies use various metrics and reporting frameworks, such as the Global Reporting Initiative (GRI) or the Sustainability Accounting Standards Board (SASB), to track and disclose their CSR performance. The scope of CSR includes establishing clear metrics and transparent reporting mechanisms.

12) Global Perspective and Cultural Sensitivity:

The scope of CSR extends beyond national borders. Multinational corporations must navigate cultural differences and adapt their CSR strategies to the regions in which they operate. Understanding global issues and adapting CSR practices accordingly is essential for companies with a global footprint.

1.2 Evolution of CSR:

Corporate Social Responsibility (CSR) is a concept that has transformed significantly over time. It has evolved from a narrow focus on philanthropy and charitable activities to a comprehensive approach that encompasses environmental sustainability, ethical business practices, and social impact. This transformation reflects changing societal expectations, economic shifts, and the recognition that businesses have a broader role to play in society.

1) **Origins of CSR: Early Philanthropy:**

   The roots of CSR can be traced back to ancient civilizations where businesses and individuals engaged in acts of charity and philanthropy. However, the modern concept of CSR began to take shape during the late 19th century and early 20th century as large corporations amassed wealth and influence.

2) **Industrial Revolution and Labor Concerns:**

   The Industrial Revolution brought about significant economic growth but also raised concerns about labor conditions and worker rights. As workers faced harsh conditions in factories and mines, social reform movements gained momentum. These movements, alongside the emergence of labor unions, pushed companies to address issues related to employee welfare, workplace safety, and fair wages.

3) **The Rise of Corporate Foundations:**

   In the early 20th century, some pioneering companies established corporate foundations to formalize their philanthropic efforts. Examples include the Rockefeller Foundation and the Ford Foundation. These foundations focused on education, public health, and community development, setting a precedent for corporate involvement in societal issues.

4) **Post-World War II Era: Expanding Horizons:**

   The aftermath of World War II marked a turning point in CSR. The devastation caused by the war led to heightened awareness of the need for businesses to contribute to the rebuilding and betterment of society. Companies increasingly engaged in philanthropy and community development projects.

5) **Emergence of Environmental Concerns:**

   The 1960s and 1970s witnessed a growing environmental consciousness. Events like the publication of Rachel Carson's "Silent Spring" and the first Earth Day in 1970 galvanized public opinion around environmental issues. Companies began to face scrutiny for their environmental impact, leading to the development of environmental regulations and the birth of the modern environmental movement.

6) **Legal and Regulatory Developments:**

   The late 20th century saw government's worldwide introducing legislation to regulate business practices in areas such as environmental protection, consumer rights, and workplace safety. These regulations forced companies to consider their social and environmental responsibilities seriously.

7) **Stakeholder Theory and Beyond:**
The 1980s and 1990s brought forth stakeholder theory, which argued that businesses should consider the interests of all stakeholders, not just shareholders. This idea challenged the traditional view of companies solely existing to maximize shareholder wealth. CSR began to incorporate a broader range of stakeholders, including customers, employees, suppliers, and communities.

8) **Globalization and Supply Chain Responsibility:**
As companies expanded globally, they faced ethical challenges related to international labor practices, human rights, and environmental standards. The scope of CSR expanded to include responsible sourcing, supply chain transparency, and addressing issues in global operations.

9) **Transparency and Reporting:**
The late 20th century also witnessed the development of reporting frameworks, such as the Global Reporting Initiative (GRI) and the Dow Jones Sustainability Index. These frameworks standardized the reporting of CSR activities, making it easier for stakeholders to assess a company's social and environmental performance.

10) **The New Millennium: CSR as a Business Imperative:**
The early 21st century saw CSR evolve from a peripheral activity to a core business strategy. Companies realized that CSR could enhance their reputation, mitigate risks, and drive innovation. This shift in perspective marked the integration of CSR into business models and corporate culture.

11) **Emergence of Impact Investing and Social Entrepreneurship:**
The 21st century has witnessed the rise of impact investing, which seeks to generate both financial returns and positive social or environmental outcomes. Similarly, social entrepreneurship has gained prominence as individuals and organizations explore business models that address societal challenges.

12) **Sustainable Development Goals (SDGs):**
The United Nations' adoption of the Sustainable Development Goals in 2015 provided a universal framework for addressing global challenges. Many companies have aligned their CSR efforts with these goals, further emphasizing the interconnectedness of business and societal well-being.

13) **Evolving CSR in a Digital Age:**
The digital age has introduced new opportunities and challenges for CSR. Companies now use technology to engage with stakeholders, track environmental metrics, and promote transparency. At the same time, they face scrutiny related to data privacy, cybersecurity, and the impact of digital technologies on society.

14) **CSR in the Face of Global Crises:**

The COVID-19 pandemic highlighted the role of CSR in responding to global crises. Many companies stepped up to provide resources, support healthcare systems, and protect the well-being of their employees and communities. This crisis underscored the importance of corporate resilience and adaptability in the face of unexpected challenges.

15) **Future Trends and Challenges:**

Looking ahead, CSR is likely to continue evolving. Key trends include greater emphasis on climate action, diversity and inclusion, and ethical artificial intelligence. Companies will also face challenges related to stakeholder activism, ethical supply chain management, and the need to balance short-term financial goals with long-term sustainability.

1.3 The Evolving Role of Stakeholders:

Corporate Social Responsibility (CSR) has evolved significantly over the years, and one of the key driving forces behind this evolution has been the changing role of stakeholders.

1) **Consumers as Activists:**

Consumers are increasingly becoming conscious of a company's social and environmental practices. They wield significant power in influencing corporate behavior through their purchasing decisions. Social media and online activism have empowered consumers to hold companies accountable for their CSR commitments. Brands that align with consumer values often witness increased loyalty and support.

2) **Investors Driving Change:**

Investors are recognizing the correlation between sustainable practices and long-term financial performance. There's a growing trend of responsible investing where stakeholders consider a company's environmental, social, and governance (ESG) factors. Shareholder activism and the integration of ESG metrics into investment decisions are compelling companies to prioritize CSR initiatives to attract and retain investment.

3) **Employees as Advocates:**

Employees are increasingly seeking purpose-driven work environments. They prefer companies that prioritize CSR, fostering a sense of pride and commitment among the workforce. Engaged employees can become powerful advocates for a company's CSR efforts, positively impacting brand image and attracting top talent.

4) **Government Regulations and Policies:**

Governments worldwide are imposing stricter regulations and policies concerning corporate social responsibility. These measures aim to ensure that companies operate ethically, reduce their environmental impact, and contribute positively to society. Compliance with these regulations has become essential for businesses, influencing their CSR strategies.

5) **NGOs and Civil Society:**
Non-governmental organizations (NGOs) and civil society play a crucial role in advocating for social and environmental causes. They often collaborate with businesses to drive meaningful CSR initiatives. Their expertise, networks, and credibility in addressing societal issues make them valuable partners for companies aiming to make a tangible impact.

6) **Supply Chain Partnerships:**
Companies are recognizing the importance of extending their CSR initiatives across their supply chains. Collaborating with suppliers to ensure ethical sourcing, fair labor practices, and environmental sustainability throughout the supply chain has become a key focus. Partnerships and transparency within the supply chain are vital in achieving comprehensive CSR goals.

7) **Local Communities Engagement:**
Businesses are increasingly involving local communities in their CSR endeavor. Collaborative projects focusing on community development, education, healthcare, and environmental conservation not only benefit the society but also enhance the company's reputation and relationships within the community.

8) **Media and Public Opinion:**
Media coverage significantly influences public perception of a company's CSR efforts. Positive coverage of impactful CSR initiatives can enhance brand reputation, while negative publicity due to irresponsible practices can severely damage it. Companies are now more sensitive to public opinion and strive to communicate their CSR activities effectively.

9) **Technology and Innovation:**
Advancements in technology have provided innovative solutions for addressing social and environmental issues. Companies leverage technology for sustainable practices, such as renewable energy adoption, waste reduction, and developing products with lower environmental footprints, showcasing their commitment to CSR.

10) **Education and Awareness Campaigns:**
Companies engage in educational campaigns to raise awareness about social and environmental issues. These initiatives aim to educate stakeholders; including consumers, employees, and the general public, fostering a culture of responsibility and encouraging informed choices.

11) **Supplier and Investor Transparency:**
Stakeholders demand greater transparency regarding CSR practices. Companies are expected to disclose comprehensive reports on their CSR activities, including environmental impact assessments, labor practices, and community engagement efforts. Transparency builds trust and credibility among stakeholders.

12) **Long-term Sustainability Goals:**
Stakeholders increasingly prioritize companies with long-term sustainability goals. Beyond short-term philanthropic activities, there's a focus on integrating CSR into the core business strategy. Aligning CSR initiatives with business objectives ensures sustained impact, fostering stakeholder confidence and support.

1.4 CSR towards Stakeholders:

Corporate Social Responsibility (CSR) involves a company's commitment to operating ethically and contributing positively to society. When it comes to stakeholders, CSR efforts aim to benefit various groups beyond just shareholders. Here's a breakdown of CSR towards different stakeholders:

1) **Employees**:
Companies ensure fair wages, equitable benefits, and opportunities for professional growth. They create safe, inclusive workplaces that promote a healthy work-life balance. This involves implementing diversity and inclusion programs and offering initiatives like flexible working hours or remote work options. Employee well-being is a priority, fostering a positive and productive work culture.

2) **Customers**:
Businesses prioritize delivering high-quality products/services while maintaining transparent and ethical practices. They actively seek and integrate customer feedback to improve offerings, ensuring that they address customer needs effectively. Transparency in marketing, pricing, and product information builds trust and fosters strong, long-term relationships with customers.

3) **Communities**:
Companies engage with communities by supporting local initiatives, charities, and development projects. They invest in education, healthcare, and infrastructure, positively impacting the areas where they operate. Volunteer programs and partnerships with local organizations demonstrate a commitment to community welfare and sustainable development, aiming to create lasting positive change.

4) **Suppliers and Partners**:
Businesses establish fair trade practices and prioritize ethical sourcing throughout their supply chain. They maintain respectful relationships with suppliers and partners, ensuring that sustainability practices are integrated into operations. Collaboration for mutual benefit involves sharing sustainable goals and working together to implement environmentally friendly and socially responsible strategies.

5) **Environment**:
Companies focus on reducing their environmental impact by adopting sustainable practices. This involves minimizing carbon emissions, conserving resources, and implementing waste reduction strategies. Investments in renewable energy sources

and the adoption of eco-friendly technologies are integral parts of the commitment to environmental stewardship.

6) **Shareholders/Investors**:

Businesses prioritize transparency in financial reporting and governance, aligning their strategies with long-term sustainability goals. They demonstrate a commitment to ethical conduct and consider the environmental and social impact of their decisions, aiming to create sustainable value for shareholders while balancing short-term returns with long-term viability.

1.5 CSR Policy and Governance:

Insurance products and services encompass a wide range of offerings designed to mitigate financial risks and provide protection to individuals, businesses, and assets. These offerings include life insurance, which provides financial security to beneficiaries in the event of the policyholder's death; health insurance, which covers medical expenses and healthcare-related costs; property and casualty insurance, protecting against damage to property and liability for injuries or damages; auto insurance, ensuring financial coverage in case of accidents or theft; and various specialized policies such as disability insurance, travel insurance, and pet insurance, all tailored to address specific risks and needs. Insurance services extend beyond policy issuance to include claims processing, risk assessment, policy customization, and advisory services, helping individuals and organizations make informed decisions to safeguard their financial well-being and peace of mind.

1.5.1 Policy of CSR:

Corporate Social Responsibility (CSR) has become a cornerstone of modern business practice. As companies face increasing pressure to address environmental, social, and ethical challenges, the development and implementation of CSR policies have become imperative. Corporate Social Responsibility (CSR) policies are formalized sets of guidelines, principles, and commitments that outline a company's approach to conducting its business in a socially responsible and ethical manner. These policies serve as a roadmap, guiding a company's actions, decisions, and strategies to align with the values of sustainability, environmental stewardship, social responsibility, and ethical conduct. CSR policies go beyond profit generation and emphasize the broader impact a company has on society and the environment.

A) The Significance of CSR Policies:

Following are the significance of CSR policies:

1) **Ethical Framework**:

CSR policies establish an ethical framework for a company's operations. They define the company's values, principles, and standards of conduct, fostering a culture of integrity and responsibility.

2) **Stakeholder Expectations**:

In today's business landscape, stakeholders, including customers, employees, investors, and communities, expect companies to demonstrate a commitment to CSR. CSR policies help meet these expectations and build trust with stakeholders.

3) **Risk Mitigation**:

CSR policies help identify and mitigate risks associated with unethical or unsustainable practices. By addressing potential risks upfront, companies can prevent reputational damage, legal issues, and financial losses.

4) **Competitive Advantage**:

Companies that embrace CSR can gain a competitive advantage. CSR policies can drive innovation, enhance brand reputation, and attract socially conscious customers, investors, and talent.

5) **Legal Compliance**:

`CSR policies ensure that a company complies with relevant laws, regulations, and industry standards related to environmental, social, and ethical issues. This helps prevent legal and regulatory issues.

B) **Key Components of Effective CSR Policies:**

A well-structured CSR policy should encompass several key components:

1) **Vision and Mission**:

Clearly state the company's vision and mission regarding CSR. This sets the overall direction and purpose of CSR initiatives within the organization.

2) **Stakeholder Engagement**:

Define how the company will engage with and consider the interests of various stakeholders, including employees, customers, investors, suppliers, communities, and NGOs.

3) **Ethical Principles**:

Specify the ethical principles and values that guide the company's behavior, emphasizing honesty, transparency, fairness, and integrity.

4) **Environmental Commitments**:

Detail the company's environmental commitments, including goals for reducing environmental impact, conserving resources, and adopting sustainable practices.

5) **Social Initiatives**:

Describe the company's efforts to support social causes, such as diversity and inclusion, employee well-being, philanthropy, and community development.

6) **Compliance and Governance**:

Explain how the company ensures compliance with relevant laws and regulations, as well as how it maintains transparency in CSR reporting.

7) **Measurement and Reporting**:
Define key performance indicators (KPIs) and metrics used to measure CSR performance. Specify the frequency and channels for reporting CSR data.

8) **Continuous Improvement**:
Emphasize the company's commitment to continuous improvement in CSR efforts through regular assessments, feedback mechanisms, and adjustments to policies and practices.

D) Best Practices in Crafting CSR Policies:

To create effective CSR policies, businesses can follow these best practices:

1) **Alignment with Business Strategy:**
Ensure that CSR policies align with the company's overall business strategy, values, and long-term goals. Integration of CSR into the core business strategy ensures sustainability.

2) **Engagement of Leadership:**
Secure active support and commitment from senior leadership, including the CEO and board of directors. Leadership buy-in is crucial for the success of CSR efforts.

3) **Integration into Operations**:
Embed CSR practices into core business operations rather than treating them as separate initiatives. Make CSR part of the company's DNA.

4) **Regular Reporting**:
Publish regular and transparent CSR reports that highlight progress, achievements, and areas for improvement. Reporting builds accountability and transparency.

5) **Stakeholder Collaboration:**
Collaborate closely with stakeholders to understand their expectations and concerns and incorporate their input into CSR initiatives. Engage in two-way communication.

6) **Global Considerations**:
Consider the global nature of CSR, addressing international standards and local context-specific issues. Recognize cultural differences and adapt CSR practices accordingly.

7) **Measurable Goals**:
Set specific, measurable, achievable, relevant, and time-bound (SMART) goals for CSR initiatives. Goals provide clarity and direction.

8) **Monitoring and Evaluation:**
Regularly monitor and evaluate CSR initiatives to measure their impact and effectiveness. Use data to inform decision-making and improvements.

9) **Adaptability:**
Be flexible and adaptive in responding to emerging CSR issues and evolving stakeholder expectations. Stay attuned to societal and environmental changes.

E) Illustrative Examples of CSR Policies:

Following are the examples of CSR policies:

1) Environmental Stewardship:

A technology company's CSR policy may include commitments to reduce carbon emissions, increase energy efficiency, and minimize waste. It could set targets for using renewable energy sources and implementing green building practices.

2) Diversity and Inclusion:

A multinational corporation's CSR policy may emphasize diversity and inclusion by committing to a diverse workforce and inclusive workplace practices. It may outline initiatives for gender equity, equal pay, and underrepresented minority recruitment.

3) Community Engagement:

A retail company's CSR policy may focus on community engagement. It could include commitments to support local communities through charitable donations, employee volunteer programs, and partnerships with local nonprofits.

4) Ethical Sourcing:

A fashion brand's CSR policy might address ethical sourcing. It may require suppliers to adhere to fair labor practices, avoid child labor, and use sustainable materials. The policy might also outline auditing and monitoring procedures.

5) Transparency and Reporting:

A financial institution's CSR policy could emphasize transparency and reporting. It might commit to providing regular CSR reports that detail the company's financial contributions to social and environmental causes, as well as its impact on communities.

1.5.2 Governance of CSR:

Corporate Social Responsibility (CSR) governance is a critical aspect of modern business practice. It encompasses the structures, processes, and mechanisms that companies establish to oversee, implement, and manage their CSR initiatives effectively. CSR governance refers to the systems and processes that guide a company's CSR activities and ensure that they align with the company's values, goals, and ethical standards. It involves the establishment of clear accountability, responsibility, and oversight mechanisms to drive CSR initiatives, monitor performance, and report on outcomes. CSR governance serves as the backbone of a company's commitment to ethical, sustainable, and socially responsible business practices.

B) The Significance of CSR Governance:

Following are the significance of CSR governance:

1) Accountability:

CSR governance establishes clear lines of accountability within an organization, ensuring that responsibility for CSR initiatives is assigned and monitored.

2) **Risk Management**:

Effective CSR governance helps identify and mitigate CSR-related risks, including reputational, legal, and operational risks. It minimizes the potential negative impact of irresponsible practices.

3) **Stakeholder Engagement:**

It facilitates meaningful engagement with stakeholders, including employees, customers, investors, suppliers, and communities, by ensuring that their perspectives are considered in CSR decision-making.

4) **Compliance and Transparency**: CSR governance ensures that the company complies with relevant laws, regulations, and industry standards related to CSR. It also promotes transparency in CSR reporting.

5) **Performance Measurement:**

It establishes systems for measuring CSR performance, enabling the company to assess progress toward goals and objectives, and make informed decisions based on data.

6) **Continuous Improvement:**

CSR governance encourages continuous improvement in CSR efforts by incorporating feedback mechanisms, regular assessments, and adjustments to policies and practices.

C) **Key Components of Effective CSR Governance:**

A well-structured CSR governance framework should encompass several key components:

1) **Board of Directors and Leadership**:

The board of directors should include members who understand and support CSR objectives. In some cases, a dedicated CSR committee within the board may be responsible for overseeing CSR activities.

2) **CSR Manager or Department**:

Many companies appoint a dedicated CSR manager or establish a CSR department responsible for coordinating and implementing CSR initiatives. This team collaborates with various departments and stakeholders to ensure alignment with CSR goals.

3) **Stakeholder Engagement**:

CSR governance includes mechanisms for engaging with stakeholders, such as regular meetings, surveys, and feedback mechanisms. This helps in understanding stakeholders' concerns and expectations.

4) **Risk Management**:

Companies should identify and assess CSR-related risks, including reputational, legal, and operational risks. Develop strategies to mitigate these risks.

5) **Compliance and Reporting**:
Establish processes for ensuring compliance with CSR policies, laws, and regulations. Develop a system for collecting, analyzing, and reporting CSR data internally and externally.

6) **Performance Measurement**:
Define key performance indicators (KPIs) and benchmarks to measure CSR performance. Regularly assess progress and make adjustments as needed.

7) **Training and Awareness**:
Provide training and raise awareness among employees about CSR policies and practices. Encourage a culture of responsibility and sustainability.

8) **Supply Chain Management**:
Integrate CSR considerations into supply chain management by evaluating suppliers' ethical and environmental practices and promoting responsible sourcing.

9) **Communication and Transparency**:
Communicate CSR efforts and achievements to internal and external stakeholders through various channels, such as annual CSR reports, websites, and social media.

10) **Continuous Improvement**:
Continuously evaluate and improve CSR governance structures and processes to adapt to changing CSR trends and challenges.

D) Best Practices in CSR Governance:

To establish effective CSR governance, businesses can follow these best practices:

1) **Alignment with Business Strategy:**
Ensure that CSR governance aligns with the company's overall business strategy, values, and long-term goals. Integration of CSR into the core business strategy ensures sustainability.

2) **Engagement of Leadership:**
Secure active support and commitment from senior leadership, including the CEO and board of directors. Leadership buy-in is crucial for the success of CSR governance.

3) **Integration into Operations:**
Embed CSR practices into core business operations rather than treating them as separate initiatives. Make CSR part of the company's DNA.

4) **Regular Reporting:**
Publish regular and transparent CSR reports that highlight progress, achievements, and areas for improvement. Reporting builds accountability and transparency.

5) **Stakeholder Collaboration:**
Collaborate closely with stakeholders to understand their expectations and concerns and incorporate their input into CSR initiatives. Engage in two-way communication.

6) **Global Considerations:**

Consider the global nature of CSR, addressing international standards and local context-specific issues. Recognize cultural differences and adapt CSR practices accordingly.

7) **Measurable Goals:**

Set specific, measurable, achievable, relevant, and time-bound (SMART) goals for CSR initiatives. Goals provide clarity and direction.

8) **Monitoring and Evaluation:**

Regularly monitor and evaluate CSR initiatives to measure their impact and effectiveness. Use data to inform decision-making and improvements.

9) **Adaptability:**

Be flexible and adaptive in responding to emerging CSR issues and evolving stakeholder expectations. Stay attuned to societal and environmental changes.

E) **Illustrative Examples of CSR Governance:**

Following are the examples of CSR governance:

1) **Board Oversight:**

A company's board of directors establishes a CSR committee responsible for overseeing CSR activities. This committee sets the strategic direction for CSR, reviews progress, and ensures alignment with the company's values and goals.

2) **Dedicated CSR Department:**

A multinational corporation establishes a dedicated CSR department headed by a Chief Sustainability Officer (CSO). This department collaborates with various divisions within the company to implement CSR initiatives, monitor performance, and report results.

3) **Stakeholder Engagement Council:**

An automotive manufacturer forms a stakeholder engagement council consisting of representatives from various stakeholder groups, including employees, customers, suppliers, and environmental organizations. This council provides input, feedback, and recommendations on CSR initiatives.

4) **Supplier Auditing:**

A fashion retailer includes supplier auditing as part of its CSR governance. It conducts regular audits of suppliers to ensure they adhere to ethical labor practices, environmental standards, and responsible sourcing guidelines.

5) **Environmental Risk Assessment:**

An energy company conducts an environmental risk assessment as a component of CSR governance. This assessment identifies potential environmental risks associated with its operations, enabling the company to develop risk mitigation strategies.

F) The Impact of Effective CSR Governance:

Effective CSR governance has far-reaching impacts on a company's performance, reputation, and contribution to society:

1) **Enhanced Reputation:**

   Companies with robust CSR governance often enjoy enhanced reputations, which can attract socially conscious customers, investors, and talent.

2) **Risk Mitigation:**

   CSR governance helps identify and mitigate CSR-related risks, minimizing the potential negative impact on a company's bottom line and reputation.

3) **Competitive Advantage:**

   Businesses with effective CSR governance can gain a competitive advantage by innovating in sustainability, building brand loyalty, and meeting stakeholder expectations.

4) **Improved Stakeholder Relations:**

   CSR governance fosters improved relations with stakeholders by demonstrating commitment to their interests, needs, and concerns.

5) **Sustainable Growth:**

   CSR governance supports long-term sustainability by ensuring that CSR initiatives align with the company's strategic goals and values.

6) **Contribution to Society:**

   Companies with effective CSR governance can make a positive contribution to society by addressing pressing environmental and social challenges.

1.6 Theories and Models of CSR:

Corporate Social Responsibility (CSR) encompasses various theories and models that guide how businesses engage with ethical, social, and environmental responsibilities alongside their economic objectives. Classical models, such as Carroll's CSR Pyramid and Friedman's Shareholder Theory, emphasize economic profit as the primary goal but recognize additional layers of responsibility. Contemporary models, including the Triple Bottom Line, Stakeholder Theory, Corporate Citizenship, and Sustainable Development, broaden the focus to encompass environmental, social, and stakeholder interests. These models reflect the evolution of CSR from a narrow profit-centric approach to a holistic perspective, where businesses recognize their roles in addressing global challenges, building meaningful stakeholder relationships, and contributing to a sustainable and socially responsible future.

1.6.1 Caroll's CSR Pyramids:

Carroll's CSR Pyramid is a well-known framework in the field of corporate social responsibility (CSR) that was developed by Archie B. Carroll in 1991. It provides a comprehensive perspective on the various responsibilities that organizations have towards society.

1) **Economic Responsibility:**

   At the base of the pyramid lies economic responsibility, this is the foundational obligation of any business. Organizations must generate profit, sustain growth, and create value for shareholders and stakeholders. This involves efficient resource allocation, cost management, and competitiveness in the market.

2) **Legal Responsibility:**

   Above economic responsibility, organizations are required to operate within the boundaries of the law. Compliance with local, national, and international regulations is essential to maintain ethical and legal standing. This includes adhering to environmental laws, labor standards, and consumer protection regulations.

3) **Ethical Responsibility:**

   Ethical responsibility goes beyond legal obligations. It involves conducting business with integrity, fairness, and honesty. Ethical behavior includes avoiding discriminatory practices, respecting human rights, and promoting diversity and inclusion within the organization.

4) **Philanthropic Responsibility:**

   The second tier of Carroll's pyramid includes philanthropic responsibilities, which represent an organization's discretionary efforts to give back to society. This may include charitable donations, community involvement, and volunteer programs. These actions are not mandated by law or required for business survival but contribute positively to the organization's reputation.

5) **Stakeholder Perspective:**

   Throughout the pyramid, Carroll emphasizes the importance of considering the interests of stakeholders. Organizations should identify and engage with their various stakeholders, including customers, employees, suppliers, investors, communities, and government bodies. Understanding stakeholder concerns helps in addressing CSR effectively.

6) **Balancing Act:**

   Carroll's framework recognizes that there is a delicate balance between the four components of the pyramid. Organizations must balance their economic pursuits with legal compliance, ethical behavior, and philanthropic endeavors. This balance is crucial for sustainable business practices.

7) **Hierarchy of Priorities:**

   The pyramid signifies a hierarchy of priorities. Economic and legal responsibilities are considered primary because they are essential for business survival. Ethical and philanthropic responsibilities come after the first two tiers are satisfied.

8) **Voluntary Nature:**
Ethical and philanthropic responsibilities are considered voluntary because organizations are not legally obligated to engage in them. However, they can significantly enhance an organization's reputation and contribute to long-term success.

9) **Long-Term Perspective:**
Carroll's CSR Pyramid emphasizes the long-term perspective of CSR. It suggests that CSR is not just a short-term marketing or PR strategy but a fundamental aspect of an organization's identity and strategy.

10) **Reputation and Trust:**
Engaging in ethical and philanthropic activities can build trust and goodwill with stakeholders. A positive reputation can lead to increased customer loyalty, employee satisfaction, and investor confidence.

11) **Adaptation to Context:**
The pyramid is adaptable to different industries, regions, and cultures. CSR priorities may vary based on the nature of the business and the societal context in which it operates. Organizations should tailor their CSR efforts to align with their specific circumstances.

12) **Evolution of CSR:**
Carroll's CSR Pyramid has evolved over time. While the core principles remain relevant, the modern business landscape has seen an increased emphasis on sustainability, environmental responsibility, and social impact. Organizations may need to expand their CSR efforts to address emerging challenges and stakeholder expectations.

1.6.2 Stakeholder Theory:

Corporate Social Responsibility (CSR) has become a central concern for businesses globally, with growing expectations that organizations should contribute positively to society beyond their profit-seeking objectives. At the heart of the CSR discourse is the Stakeholder Theory, a framework that shifts the focus from the exclusive interests of shareholders to encompass the needs and concerns of all stakeholders associated with an organization. This theory recognizes that businesses do not operate in isolation but are intricately linked to a web of relationships that involve employees, customers, suppliers, communities, and more.

1) **Introduction to Stakeholder Theory:**
The Stakeholder Theory of CSR is a fundamental framework that challenges the traditional view of business as solely profit-oriented and shareholder-centric. It posits that businesses have a broader social and ethical responsibility to consider the interests of all stakeholders involved in or affected by their operations.

Stakeholders encompass a wide range of individuals and groups, including employees, customers, suppliers, communities, shareholders, and even the environment.

2) **Origins and Evolution:**

The origins of the Stakeholder Theory can be traced back to the 1960s and 1970s when the prevailing belief in shareholder primacy was increasingly questioned. Notable scholars such as R. Edward Freeman, who authored "Strategic Management: A Stakeholder Approach" in 1984, played a pivotal role in articulating and popularizing this theory. Over time, the theory has evolved to address the changing dynamics of the business environment and societal expectations.

3) **Stakeholder Identification:**

One of the core tenets of the Stakeholder Theory is the identification and recognition of stakeholders. Businesses must actively identify and categorize their stakeholders, understanding their needs, interests, and concerns. This process involves mapping out all parties who have a stake in or can affect the organization, thereby creating a comprehensive stakeholder map.

4) **Stakeholder Salience:**

Stakeholder salience is the concept that not all stakeholders are equal in terms of their influence and importance to the organization. Freeman introduced a three-dimensional model of stakeholder salience, considering attributes such as power, legitimacy, and urgency. High salience stakeholders are those with a significant impact, legitimate claims, and pressing concerns, thus warranting greater attention.

5) **The Triple Bottom Line:**

The Stakeholder Theory aligns with the Triple Bottom Line (TBL) concept, which emphasizes that businesses should measure success based on three key dimensions: economic, social, and environmental. While economic performance remains crucial, the TBL recognizes the significance of social and environmental factors in assessing an organization's overall impact.

6) **Ethical Considerations:**

Ethics play a central role in the Stakeholder Theory. It advocates for ethical decision-making and actions, emphasizing fairness, honesty, and integrity in all dealings with stakeholders. Ethical behavior fosters trust and goodwill, critical for building enduring relationships.

7) **Balancing Stakeholder Interests:**

A key challenge in implementing the Stakeholder Theory is balancing the often conflicting interests of various stakeholders. Effective stakeholder management requires businesses to navigate these conflicts diplomatically, aiming for mutually beneficial solutions and compromises.

8) **Corporate Governance:**

Stakeholder Theory has implications for corporate governance. It suggests that governance structures should be designed to represent the interests of a broader set of stakeholders beyond shareholders. This can involve the inclusion of stakeholder representatives on boards or committees.

9) **Long-Term Perspective:**

Stakeholder Theory promotes a long-term perspective in decision-making. Instead of pursuing short-term profits at the expense of stakeholders, organizations adopting this theory recognize that building strong, enduring relationships with stakeholders is essential for sustained success.

10) **Competitive Advantage:**

While some may view CSR initiatives as a cost, Stakeholder Theory argues that they can provide a competitive advantage. Positive stakeholder relationships can enhance brand reputation, customer loyalty, and employee engagement, ultimately contributing to long-term profitability.

11) **Environmental Sustainability:**

The Stakeholder Theory aligns with the growing emphasis on environmental sustainability. Recognizing the environment as a stakeholder, it encourages businesses to adopt eco-friendly practices and consider the long-term ecological impact of their operations.

1.6.3 Triple Bottom Line Theory (TBL):

Corporate Social Responsibility (CSR) has evolved significantly over the years, expanding beyond traditional profit-centric models to encompass a broader perspective of business success. The Triple Bottom Line (TBL) theory, introduced by John Elkington in the 1990s, represents a paradigm shift in how organizations assess their performance. Instead of focusing solely on financial profit, the TBL theory calls for the evaluation of three critical dimensions: economic, social, and environmental. This comprehensive examination of the TBL theory aims to provide a detailed insight into its key principles, historical evolution, practical applications, criticisms, and real-world examples.

1) **Introduction to the Triple Bottom Line (TBL) Theory:**

The TBL theory is a paradigm-shifting framework in the field of Corporate Social Responsibility (CSR). It suggests that businesses should not only measure their success based on financial profit (the "bottom line") but also consider their impact on society and the environment. The three "bottom lines" are economic, social, and environmental.

2) Historical Context and Emergence:

The TBL theory was introduced by John Elkington in the 1990s as a response to the changing dynamics of the business world. It emerged as recognition that traditional financial metrics alone were insufficient for assessing the overall performance of organizations. Instead, it emphasized the need to account for broader social and environmental dimensions.

3) Economic Bottom Line:

The economic bottom line represents the financial performance of an organization. It includes traditional financial measures such as revenue, profit, and return on investment. In the TBL framework, economic sustainability involves maintaining profitability and financial stability while creating value for shareholders.

4) Social Bottom Line:

The social bottom line focuses on the impact of an organization's operations on society and its stakeholders. This dimension considers factors like employee well-being, community engagement, and the organization's contributions to social welfare. Social sustainability involves practices that enhance the quality of life for individuals and communities.

5) Environmental Bottom Line:

The environmental bottom line assesses an organization's impact on the natural environment. It encompasses activities related to resource conservation, pollution prevention, and sustainable practices. Environmental sustainability involves minimizing harm to the planet and working towards a net positive ecological impact.

6) Interconnectedness of the Bottom Lines:

A fundamental principle of the TBL theory is that these three bottom lines are interconnected and interdependent. Achieving success in one dimension should not come at the expense of the others. For instance, a focus on short-term economic gains should not harm social or environmental sustainability in the long run.

7) Measurement and Reporting:

To implement the TBL theory, organizations must develop metrics and reporting mechanisms that capture their performance in each of the three dimensions. This often involves developing sustainability reports or integrated reporting that provide stakeholders with a holistic view of the organization's impact.

8) Stakeholder Engagement:

Stakeholder engagement is a critical aspect of the TBL theory. It encourages organizations to actively involve stakeholders in decision-making processes related to economic, social, and environmental matters. Engaging stakeholders helps in understanding their concerns and aligning business practices with societal expectations.

9) **Triple P Approach: People, Planet & Profit:**

The TBL is sometimes referred to as the "Triple P" approach, emphasizing the importance of People, Planet, and Profit. This framework guides organizations to balance the interests of all three dimensions, recognizing that they are interconnected and collectively contribute to sustainable success.

10) **Corporate Responsibility and Ethics:**

The TBL theory inherently promotes corporate responsibility and ethical behavior. It encourages organizations to act in ways that are socially and environmentally responsible, reflecting a commitment to ethical principles and values.

11) **Innovation and Competitive Advantage:**

Implementing the TBL theory can drive innovation. Organizations that adopt sustainable practices often find opportunities for cost savings, new markets, and improved brand reputation. This innovation can lead to a competitive advantage in the long term.

1.6.4 Porter and Kramer's Shared Value Theory:

Porter and Kramer's Shared Value Theory redefines the role of business by advocating for the simultaneous creation of economic and social value. It challenges the traditional view that CSR is separate from core business strategy and asserts that companies can address societal issues while enhancing their competitiveness and profitability. This theory emphasizes the integration of social and economic goals, the expansion of stakeholder considerations, and the development of new metrics to measure shared value. By aligning business objectives with societal needs, Shared Value Theory provides a framework for organizations to contribute positively to society while securing long-term financial success, ultimately reshaping the way businesses engage with social and environmental challenges.

1) **Introduction to Shared Value Theory:**

Porter and Kramer's Shared Value Theory is a groundbreaking framework in the field of Corporate Social Responsibility (CSR) and business strategy. It challenges the traditional view that CSR is a separate philanthropic activity and proposes that businesses can simultaneously create economic value for themselves and social value for society. This comprehensive examination delves into the core principles, historical context, practical applications, criticisms, and examples of Shared Value Theory.

2) **Historical Context and Emergence:**

Shared Value Theory was introduced by Michael Porter and Mark Kramer in their seminal 2011 article, "Creating Shared Value." It emerged as a response to the limitations of traditional CSR, which often treated social and environmental issues as external to a company's core business strategy. Shared Value Theory emerged at a time when there was increasing scrutiny on the role of business in addressing pressing societal challenges.

3) **Redefining the Role of Business:**
At its core, Shared Value Theory redefines the role of business in society. It goes beyond the notion that businesses should merely minimize harm (do no harm) or engage in philanthropy (give back). Instead, it asserts that businesses should actively seek opportunities to create measurable, positive social and environmental impact while simultaneously enhancing their competitiveness and profitability

4) **Integration of Social and Economic Goals:**
One of the fundamental principles of Shared Value Theory is the integration of social and economic goals. It rejects the notion of trade-offs between profitability and societal impact, suggesting that the two can be mutually reinforcing. Businesses are encouraged to identify areas where addressing societal needs aligns with their core business strategies.

5) **Expanding the Scope of Stakeholders:**
Shared Value Theory recognizes that businesses have a broad set of stakeholders, which includes not only shareholders but also customers, employees, suppliers, communities, and governments. It encourages businesses to consider the interests of all these stakeholders and find ways to create value for them.

6) **Business Models for Shared Value:**
To implement Shared Value Theory, organizations must rethink their business models. This may involve identifying new market opportunities in addressing unmet societal needs, reducing operational inefficiencies, or creating innovative products and services that solve social and environmental problems while driving revenue growth.

7) **Measuring Shared Value:**
Measuring Shared Value is a crucial aspect of the theory. Porter and Kramer advocate for the development of new metrics that capture both economic and social impact. These metrics should be integrated into an organization's reporting mechanisms to provide a comprehensive view of its performance.

8) **Examples of Shared Value in Practice:**
Numerous companies have successfully implemented Shared Value strategies. Nestlé, for instance, created a shared value initiative in which it committed to improving the nutritional value of its products while increasing market share in emerging economies. This approach aligned social goals (improving nutrition) with economic goals (market growth).

9) **Healthcare and Pharmaceutical Sector:**
The healthcare and pharmaceutical sector offers a compelling example of Shared Value Theory in action. Companies like Novartis have developed business models

that create shared value by addressing global health challenges. Novartis's Access to Medicine initiative focuses on providing essential medicines to underserved populations while generating revenue in low-income markets.

10) **Environmental Sustainability:**

Shared Value Theory aligns with the growing emphasis on environmental sustainability. Companies like Unilever have made sustainability a core part of their business strategy. Unilever's Sustainable Living Plan aims to reduce its environmental footprint while increasing revenue through sustainable product offerings.

12) **Future Potential and Global Impact:**

Despite criticisms, Shared Value Theory represents a significant shift in how businesses approach CSR and sustainability. It offers a framework for creating sustainable competitive advantages while addressing pressing societal issues. The theory has the potential to drive substantial global impact by encouraging businesses to play a more proactive and integrated role in solving complex societal challenges.

1.6.5 ISO 26000:

ISO 26000, a globally recognized standard for Corporate Social Responsibility (CSR), provides a comprehensive framework for organizations of all sizes and sectors to understand, implement, and integrate responsible business practices. Published by the International Organization for Standardization (ISO) in 2010, ISO 26000 is founded on seven core principles and addresses seven core subjects, ranging from human rights and labor practices to environmental stewardship and community engagement. This standard emphasizes stakeholder engagement, encourages the alignment of CSR with an organization's mission and values, and promotes the transparent measurement and reporting of CSR performance. ISO 26000's holistic approach to CSR seeks to enhance corporate accountability, foster ethical behavior, and empower organizations to contribute positively to society and the environment while simultaneously improving their own long-term sustainability and competitiveness on a global scale.

1) **Introduction to ISO 26000:**

ISO 26000 is a globally recognized standard that provides guidance on Corporate Social Responsibility (CSR). Published by the International Organization for Standardization (ISO) in 2010, it offers a comprehensive framework for organizations to understand and implement socially responsible practices. ISO 26000 is designed to help businesses integrate CSR into their strategies and operations, promoting ethical behavior, sustainability, and a positive impact on society.

2) **Historical Context:**

The development of ISO 26000 was influenced by the growing importance of CSR in the late 20th century. Increasing awareness of environmental and social issues, coupled with public demands for corporate accountability, led to the need for a standardized approach to CSR. ISO 26000 emerged as a response to these trends, aiming to provide organizations with a globally accepted reference for responsible business practices.

3) **Scope and Applicability:**

ISO 26000 is applicable to organizations of all sizes and sectors, both in the public and private sectors. It recognizes that CSR considerations may vary depending on an organization's size, location, and nature of its activities. Therefore, it offers flexibility to adapt to different contexts while maintaining a common foundation for CSR principles.

4) **Seven Core Principles:**

ISO 26000 is based on seven core principles that underpin CSR:

a) **Accountability:**

Organizations are accountable for their impact on society and the environment.

b) **Transparency:**

Transparency is essential in communication about CSR actions and impacts.

c) **Ethical behavior:**

Ethical behavior should guide an organization's actions in all CSR matters.

d) **Respect for stakeholder interests:**

Organizations should consider and respect the interests of their stakeholders.

e) **Respect for the rule of law:**

Compliance with laws and regulations is a fundamental aspect of CSR.

f) **Respect for international norms of behavior:**

Organizations are encouraged to follow international norms and standards.

g) **Respect for human rights:**

Organizations should respect and promote human rights in all their activities.

5) **Core Subjects and Issues:**

ISO 26000 provides guidance on seven core subjects, each containing specific issues related to CSR. These core subjects encompass a wide range of CSR considerations, including organizational governance, human rights, labor practices, the environment, fair operating practices, consumer issues, and community involvement. Organizations are encouraged to assess which subjects and issues are most relevant to their specific context.

6) **Integration into Organizational Practices:**

A key emphasis of ISO 26000 is the integration of CSR into an organization's practices and culture. This involves aligning CSR with the organization's mission, values, and core strategies. It encourages top-level leadership engagement and the establishment of CSR policies and objectives that guide decision-making at all levels.

7) **Stakeholder Engagement:**

ISO 26000 places significant importance on stakeholder engagement. Organizations are encouraged to identify their stakeholders, understand their concerns and expectations, and engage in meaningful dialogue with them. Effective stakeholder engagement is seen as essential for assessing the organization's impact and improving its CSR practices.

8) **Guidance on Implementation:**

The standard offers guidance on how organizations can practically implement CSR. It includes steps such as identifying CSR opportunities and risks, setting objectives and targets, implementing actions, and monitoring and measuring performance. ISO 26000 emphasizes the need for continuous improvement in CSR practices.

9) **Measuring and Reporting:**

While ISO 26000 does not provide specific metrics or reporting requirements, it does stress the importance of measuring and reporting on CSR performance. Organizations are encouraged to develop their own indicators and reporting mechanisms, considering the needs of stakeholders and relevant international standards, such as the Global Reporting Initiative (GRI).

10) **Benefits of ISO 26000 Implementation:**

Implementing ISO 26000 can bring several benefits to organizations. These include enhanced reputation and trust among stakeholders, improved risk management, cost savings through efficiency gains, increased market access, and the ability to attract and retain socially responsible investors and customers.

11) **Criticisms and Challenges:**

ISO 26000 is not without criticisms. Some argue that it lacks specificity and may be seen as too vague or non-binding. Others question the effectiveness of voluntary standards in driving meaningful CSR practices, especially in industries or regions where regulatory frameworks are weak.

12) **Global Impact and Future Relevance:**

ISO 26000 has had a significant global impact by raising awareness of CSR and providing a common reference point for organizations worldwide. Its relevance is expected to continue growing as CSR becomes increasingly integral to business strategy and as stakeholders, including investors and consumers, demand greater transparency and responsibility from organizations.

1.6.6 Corporate Citizenship Models:

Corporate Citizenship Models of CSR represent a comprehensive approach to corporate social responsibility, viewing businesses as ethical and social actors within society rather than solely as profit-driven entities. Rooted in the metaphor of corporate citizenship, this framework emphasizes the interdependence between businesses and their societal environments. It encompasses three key dimensions: economic responsibilities (profit generation), legal responsibilities (compliance with laws and regulations), and ethical and philanthropic responsibilities (ethical behavior and community engagement). Stakeholder engagement, sustainability, ethical leadership, and long-term thinking are integral components. While critics argue about potential idealism and insincerity, the model's future lies in aligning profit motives with ethical and societal concerns, responding to evolving stakeholder expectations for responsible corporate behavior.

1) Introduction to Corporate Citizenship Models of CSR:

Corporate Social Responsibility (CSR) has evolved significantly, and one prominent framework is the Corporate Citizenship model. This model emphasizes that businesses are not just economic entities but also citizens of society with ethical and social responsibilities. In this comprehensive examination, we delve into the core concepts, historical evolution, key principles, practical applications, and criticisms of the Corporate Citizenship Models of CSR.

2) Historical Development:

The concept of corporate citizenship has its roots in the 20th century, gaining prominence as businesses increasingly recognized their societal role beyond profit generation. Early thinkers like R. Edward Freeman, who introduced stakeholder theory, laid the foundation for this perspective. However, it wasn't until the late 20th century that the Corporate Citizenship model became more defined and mainstream, with scholars and practitioners advocating for businesses to actively contribute to society.

3) Dimensions of Corporate Citizenship:

Corporate Citizenship Models of CSR typically encompass three main dimensions:

a) Economic Responsibilities:

These are the fundamental obligations of a business to be profitable and contribute to economic development, including generating revenue, creating jobs, and providing returns to shareholders.

b) Legal Responsibilities:

Compliance with laws and regulations is essential. This dimension focuses on ensuring that the company operates within the legal framework, respecting contracts, and protecting the rights of all stakeholders.

c) **Ethical and Philanthropic Responsibilities:**

Beyond compliance with the law, businesses are expected to engage in ethical behavior and philanthropy. This includes actions such as supporting community initiatives, practicing fair trade, and promoting sustainability.

4) **Citizenship as a Metaphor:**

The Corporate Citizenship model employs the metaphor of citizenship to underscore the idea that businesses, like citizens, have both rights and responsibilities within the society in which they operate. This approach emphasizes the interdependence between a company and its environment, acknowledging that businesses thrive when society prospers.

5) **Stakeholder Engagement:**

Engaging with stakeholders is a fundamental aspect of the Corporate Citizenship model. Businesses are encouraged to identify and actively communicate with stakeholders, understanding their concerns and expectations. Effective engagement helps in building trust, addressing issues, and aligning business practices with societal needs.

6) **Triple Bottom Line (TBL) Integration:**

The Corporate Citizenship model often integrates the Triple Bottom Line (TBL) concept, emphasizing that businesses should measure their success based on three dimensions: economic, social, and environmental. This integration underscores the importance of balancing financial performance with social and environmental impact.

7) **Sustainable Business Practices:**

Sustainability is a central theme in the Corporate Citizenship model. Companies are encouraged to adopt sustainable practices that reduce their environmental footprint, promote social well-being, and ensure long-term viability. This includes efforts to minimize waste, conserve resources, and invest in renewable energy sources.

8) **Philanthropy and Community Engagement:**

Philanthropy and community engagement are key components of Corporate Citizenship. Businesses are expected to go beyond their core operations and contribute to the well-being of the communities in which they operate. This can involve financial donations, employee volunteer programs, and partnerships with non-profit organizations.

9) **Ethical Leadership and Governance:**

Ethical leadership and governance play a critical role in the Corporate Citizenship model. Companies are expected to have a strong ethical foundation, with leaders who prioritize integrity, transparency, and responsible decision-making. This includes adopting codes of conduct and ethical guidelines for employees and management.

10) **Long-Term Perspective:**

Corporate Citizenship emphasizes a long-term perspective in decision-making. Rather than focusing solely on short-term profits, businesses are encouraged to consider the lasting impact of their actions on society, the environment, and their own sustainability.

11) **Criticisms and Challenges:**

Critics of the Corporate Citizenship model argue that it may be too idealistic, especially in profit-driven corporate environments. They contend that businesses may engage in philanthropy and social initiatives primarily for PR purposes rather than genuine societal betterment. Balancing the pursuit of profit with ethical and social responsibility remains a complex challenge.

12) **Future of Corporate Citizenship:**

The Corporate Citizenship model is likely to gain further relevance as society's expectations of businesses evolve. As stakeholders, including consumers, investors, and regulators, demand greater accountability and ethical conduct, companies will need to embrace a broader societal role. The future of Corporate Citizenship lies in integrating ethical, social, and environmental considerations into the core of business strategy, thereby contributing positively to society while securing long-term success.

1.6.7 Ethical Theories:

Ethical theories underpinning Corporate Social Responsibility (CSR) provide a moral compass for businesses, guiding them in navigating the complex terrain of social and environmental responsibilities. Utilitarianism advocates maximizing overall societal happiness through CSR actions, deontology emphasizes adherence to universal moral principles, virtue ethics encourages the cultivation of ethical virtues within corporate culture, and ethics of care underscores empathy and relationships in CSR decision-making. Stakeholder theory extends ethical responsibilities beyond shareholders to all affected parties, while ethical egoism emphasizes self-interest in CSR actions. Social contract theory highlights businesses' obligations within the societal framework, and rights-based ethics emphasizes respecting and protecting stakeholder rights. Environmental ethics focuses on the moral imperative of environmental stewardship. Together, these ethical theories help organizations balance profit motives with ethical principles, fostering a more responsible and ethically grounded approach to CSR.

1) **Introduction to Ethical Theories in CSR:**

Ethical theories provide a foundational framework for understanding and practicing Corporate Social Responsibility (CSR). These theories guide businesses in making morally sound decisions that align with societal values and expectations. In this comprehensive exploration, we delve into various ethical theories that underpin

CSR, examining their core principles, historical evolution, practical applications, and potential criticisms.

2) **Utilitarianism:**
Utilitarianism is a consequentialist ethical theory that suggests actions should be evaluated based on their ability to maximize overall happiness or utility. In CSR, utilitarianism focuses on assessing the impact of business decisions on the well-being of stakeholders and society as a whole. Companies practicing CSR from a utilitarian perspective aim to generate the greatest good for the greatest number, often through actions like philanthropy, ethical supply chain management, and sustainable practices.

3) **Deontology:**
Deontology, developed by philosophers like Immanuel Kant, emphasizes the importance of ethical principles and duties in guiding moral actions. From a CSR standpoint, deontological ethics highlight the significance of adhering to moral duties and principles regardless of the outcomes. This approach encourages businesses to act in accordance with universal moral principles, such as honesty, respect for human rights, and justice, even if it means incurring short-term costs or challenges.

4) **Virtue Ethics:**
Virtue ethics, rooted in the works of Aristotle, focuses on cultivating virtuous character traits in individuals and, by extension, in organizations. In CSR, virtue ethics emphasize the importance of cultivating ethical virtues within the corporate culture. Companies striving for virtuous CSR exhibit traits like integrity, empathy, honesty, and responsibility, thereby fostering a culture of ethical behavior and social responsibility.

5) **Ethics of Care:**
The ethics of care theory emphasizes the significance of relationships and empathy in moral decision-making. In CSR, this theory underscores the importance of businesses caring for the well-being of their stakeholders, including employees, customers, and communities. An ethics of care approach to CSR involves practices like fair labor policies, responsible marketing, and community engagement that prioritize the welfare of vulnerable and marginalized groups.

6) **Stakeholder Theory:**
Stakeholder theory, developed by R. Edward Freeman, argues that businesses have ethical responsibilities not only to shareholders but also to all stakeholders impacted by their actions. This theory aligns with the ethical principle of justice and fairness, emphasizing that businesses should consider the interests and rights of stakeholders in their decision-making. CSR, from a stakeholder theory perspective, involves actively engaging with stakeholders, addressing their concerns, and ensuring equitable treatment.

7) **Ethical Egoism:**

Ethical egoism is a theory that asserts individuals and, by extension, organizations, should act in their self-interest. In CSR, this theory can manifest as businesses pursuing socially responsible actions primarily when it aligns with their financial interests. Critics argue that ethical egoism in CSR may lead to selective or superficial social responsibility efforts, as they are primarily motivated by profit rather than genuine moral concern.

8) **Social Contract Theory:**

Social contract theory suggests that individuals and organizations adhere to societal rules and norms based on an implicit social contract. In CSR, this theory emphasizes the importance of businesses fulfilling their societal obligations as part of this social contract. Companies are expected to operate within ethical boundaries, which may involve actions like ethical sourcing, environmental stewardship, and compliance with labor standards.

9) **Rights-Based Ethics:**

Rights-based ethics, often associated with philosophers like John Locke and John Stuart Mill, focuses on the moral rights and entitlements of individuals and organizations. In CSR, this theory asserts that businesses have an ethical duty to respect and protect the rights of all stakeholders, including employees, consumers, and the community. This involves actions like ensuring safe working conditions, respecting privacy, and upholding the right to fair treatment.

10) **Environmental Ethics:**

Environmental ethics addresses the moral responsibilities of organizations in preserving and protecting the natural environment. Businesses practicing environmental ethics in CSR recognize the intrinsic value of the environment and aim to minimize harm while promoting sustainability. This includes initiatives such as reducing carbon emissions, conserving natural resources, and supporting biodiversity conservation.

11) **The Ethical Dilemma of Profit vs. Responsibility:**

One of the central ethical dilemmas in CSR is the tension between profit motives and ethical responsibilities. Businesses often grapple with the challenge of balancing their financial goals with societal and environmental concerns. Ethical theories guide organizations in finding a harmonious equilibrium, aligning profit-seeking with moral principles and social accountability.

12) **Criticisms and Challenges:**

Ethical theories in CSR are not without criticisms and challenges. Critics argue that applying these theories can be subjective and may lead to conflicts between competing ethical principles. Additionally, some question the authenticity of CSR efforts, suggesting that businesses may engage in ethical practices for the sake of image enhancement rather than genuine moral commitment. The challenge lies in navigating these complexities and ensuring that CSR actions genuinely reflect ethical principles and societal well-being.

1.6.8 Institutional Theory:

The Institutional Theory of Corporate Social Responsibility (CSR) posits that organizations are profoundly influenced by their institutional environments, which include regulatory frameworks, societal norms, cultural values, and expectations. These institutions act as influential pillars that shape how organizations perceive and adopt CSR practices. The theory emphasizes three forms of institutional isomorphism coercive, mimetic, and normative which drive organizations to conform to prevailing CSR norms and practices. It underscores the significance of institutional pressure in determining CSR adoption and highlights the role of legitimacy in motivating organizations to engage in CSR. While providing valuable insights into the dynamics of CSR adoption, the theory has faced criticism for potentially promoting symbolic CSR actions and for not fully accounting for organizations' intrinsic ethical motivations. Nevertheless, it remains a vital framework for understanding the complex interplay between institutions and CSR practices in today's evolving societal landscape.

1) **Introduction to Institutional Theory in CSR:**
   The Institutional Theory of Corporate Social Responsibility (CSR) is a prominent framework in the study of CSR that examines how societal institutions and pressures influence the adoption and implementation of CSR practices by organizations. In this comprehensive exploration, we delve into the core concepts, historical evolution, key principles, practical applications, and criticisms of the Institutional Theory of CSR.
2) **Historical Development:**
   Institutional theory, as applied to CSR, emerged in the late 20th century, influenced by scholars like DiMaggio and Powell, who emphasized the role of institutions in shaping organizational behavior. It gained traction as CSR evolved from a peripheral concern to an integral aspect of modern business practice, reflecting changing societal expectations.
3) **Institutions as Pillars of Influence:**
   Institutional theory posits that organizations are embedded within broader institutional environments consisting of regulatory frameworks, norms, cultural values, and societal expectations. These institutions act as pillars of influence, shaping the attitudes, behaviors, and decisions of organizations, including their CSR practices.
4) **Normative, Cognitive, and Regulatory Institutions:**
   Institutional theory recognizes three main types of institutions:

a) **Normative Institutions:**

These encompass societal norms, values, and ethical standards. Normative institutions influence CSR by setting expectations regarding responsible behavior, often shaping corporate codes of conduct and ethical guidelines.

b) **Cognitive Institutions:**

Cognitive institutions refer to shared mental models, beliefs, and assumptions within society. These institutions shape how organizations perceive CSR issues, influence their strategic decisions, and determine the legitimacy of CSR initiatives.

c) **Regulatory Institutions:**

Regulatory institutions encompass laws, regulations, and governmental bodies. These institutions can mandate CSR practices through legal requirements, such as environmental regulations or labor standards.

5) **Institutional Isomorphism:**

One of the central concepts in institutional theory is institutional isomorphism, which refers to the tendency of organizations to conform to prevailing institutional norms and structures. In the context of CSR, this means that organizations often adopt CSR practices because they are considered legitimate within their institutional environment, even if those practices are not always driven by intrinsic ethical motivations.

6) **Three Forms of Isomorphism:**

Institutional theory identifies three forms of isomorphism that influence CSR adoption:

a) **Coercive Isomorphism:**

Organizations conform to CSR practices due to external pressures, such as legal mandates or regulatory requirements. They adopt CSR practices to avoid sanctions or legal consequences.

b) **Mimetic Isomorphism:**

Organizations imitate CSR practices of successful peers or competitors in their industry. They do so to gain legitimacy and avoid perceived risks, even if they may not fully understand or embrace the underlying ethical principles.

c) **Normative Isomorphism:**

Organizations adopt CSR practices because they are considered socially or ethically responsible within their institutional context. They do so to align with societal values and expectations, enhancing their reputation and stakeholder trust.

7) **The Role of Institutional Pressure:**

Institutional theory highlights the role of institutional pressure in shaping CSR practices. These pressures can be internal (within the organization) or external (from stakeholders, industry norms, or regulatory bodies). Organizations respond to these pressures by adopting CSR practices that align with institutional expectations, sometimes engaging in symbolic or symbolic-compliance CSR activities to appease stakeholders.

8) **Legitimacy and CSR:**

Legitimacy is a critical concept in institutional theory. Organizations seek to gain and maintain legitimacy by adhering to institutional norms and expectations. In the context of CSR, organizations often engage in CSR practices to enhance their legitimacy, as being seen as a responsible corporate citizen is crucial for maintaining stakeholder trust and reputation.

9) **Path Dependence:**

Path dependence is another key concept in institutional theory. It suggests that organizations' past decisions and actions influence their current behavior and choices. In the context of CSR, organizations may continue or expand their CSR initiatives based on their historical commitment to CSR or their previous success in aligning with institutional expectations.

10) **Diffusion of CSR Practices:**

Institutional theory also explores the diffusion of CSR practices within industries and sectors. As organizations observe their peers adopting CSR initiatives, they are more likely to do the same, leading to the spread of CSR practices throughout the industry. This diffusion can be driven by mimetic isomorphism.

11) **Criticisms and Challenges:**

While the Institutional Theory of CSR provides valuable insights into the influence of institutions on CSR practices, it has faced criticisms. Some argue that it may lead to "window-dressing" or superficial CSR practices driven solely by a desire for legitimacy. Additionally, it may not fully account for the motivations and intentions behind CSR actions, potentially overlooking the importance of genuine ethical commitment.

12) **Future Implications:**

The Institutional Theory of CSR highlights the role of institutions in shaping CSR practices. As societal expectations around CSR continue to evolve, organizations will need to navigate the complex interplay between institutional pressures, ethical motivations, and strategic considerations. Understanding and effectively responding to institutional influences will be crucial for organizations seeking to remain socially responsible and align their CSR practices with evolving societal norms and values.

♦♦♦

Multiple Choice Questions

1) **Corporate Social Responsibility (CSR) is a ------------ commitment by businesses to contribute to societal well-being.**
   a) Legal b) Voluntary c) Mandatory d) Arbitrary
2) **The ------------ of CSR can be traced back to philanthropic activities by early industrialists.**
   a) Initiation b) Evolution c) Negligence d) Abandonment
3) **The evolving role of stakeholders in CSR includes active participation and ------------ engagement.**
   a) Passive b) Token c) Reactive d) Proactive
4) **CSR towards stakeholders involves prioritizing the interests of ------------ affected by business operations.**
   a) Shareholders b) Competitors c) Employees d) Strangers
5) **CSR policy and governance ensure that businesses align their operations with ethical ------------.**
   a) Ambitions b) Responsibilities c) Exploitation d) Isolation
6) **------------ of CSR encompass various frameworks guiding businesses in ethical decision-making.**
   a) Principles b) Neglect c) Profit Maximization d) Secrecy
7) **The stakeholder theory asserts that businesses should consider the interests of ------------ affected by their activities.**
   a) Owners b) Employees c) All parties d) Governments
8) **The Triple Bottom Line model of CSR evaluates business success based on ------------, social, and environmental outcomes.**
   a) Economic b) Legal c) Negligence d) Arbitrary
9) **The ------------ Model suggests that businesses should contribute to societal well-being beyond profit-making.**
   a) Philanthropy b) Stakeholder c) Exploitation d) Indifference
10) **CSR policies often involve the implementation of sustainable ------------ practices.**
   a) Exploitation b) Business c) Neglect d) Development
11) **The ------------ of CSR is to create a positive impact on both society and the business.**
   a) Purpose b) Neglect c) Profit Maximization d) Secrecy
12) **The Shareholder Value Theory argues that businesses should primarily focus on maximizing returns for ------------.**
   a) Employees b) Customers c) Shareholders d) Community

13) CSR governance mechanisms include the establishment of ethical ------------ within organizations.

a) Ambitions b) Committees c) Neglect d) Consumerism

14) The ------------ Theory suggests that CSR should align with the cultural values of the community.

a) Cultural Relativism b) Profit Maximization c) Exploitation d) Arbitration

15) ------------ is an essential aspect of CSR policy, ensuring transparency and accountability.

a) Stakeholder engagement b) Philanthropy
c) Negligence d) Secrecy

16) The ------------ Model emphasizes the ethical responsibilities of businesses in their decision-making processes.

a) Stakeholder b) Exploitation c) Profit Maximization d) Neglect

17) CSR policies are designed to foster a positive impact on the ------------ and the environment.

a) Businesses b) Stakeholders c) Profits d) Negligence

18) The ------------ Model of CSR focuses on businesses balancing economic, legal, ethical, and philanthropic responsibilities.

a) Pyramid b) Exploitation c) Neglect d) Isolation

19) CSR towards stakeholders involves recognizing and addressing the ------------ of various groups.

a) Interests b) Neglect c) Profits d) Ambitions

20) The Evolutionary Model of CSR suggests that businesses progress through stages from ------------ to socially responsible.

a) Negligence b) Exploitation c) Isolation d) Unconsciousness

21) CSR policies contribute to building a positive ------------ for businesses in the eyes of the public.

a) Reputation b) Exploitation c) Neglect d) Ambitions

22) The ------------ Model of CSR emphasizes the integration of social and environmental concerns into business strategies.

a) Strategic b) Exploitation c) Neglect d) Isolation

23) CSR policies and governance mechanisms ensure that businesses operate with ------------ and integrity.

a) Transparency b) Secrecy c) Neglect d) Ambitions

24) The ------------ of CSR focus on the ethical obligations of businesses to contribute to societal well-being.

a) Goals b) Exploitation c) Neglect d) Ambitions

25) **The ------------ Model suggests that CSR should align with the long-term interests of both businesses and society.**

a) Long-term **b)** Exploitation **c)** Neglect **d)** Sustainable

Ans : **1)** b, **2)** b, **3)** d, **4)** c, **5)** b, **6)** a, **7)** c, **8)** a, **9)** b, **10)** b, **11)** a, **12)** c, **13)** b, **14)** a, **15)** a, **16)** a, **17)** b, **18)** a, **19)** a, **20)** c, **21)** a, **22)** a, **23)** a, **24)** a, **25)** d.

♦♦♦

Review Questions

Q.1. Answer the following Questions.

1) What is of Corporate Social Responsibility (CSR)? Explain the Scope of CSR.
2) Explain in detail about the Evolution of CSR.
3) Discuss about the Evolving Role of Stakeholder.
4) Write about the CSR towards Stakeholders.
4) Explain in detail about the CSR Policy.
5) Discuss about the Governance of CSR.
6) Discuss about the Carolls's CSR Pyramids.
7) Explain in detail Stakeholder Theory.
8) Write about the Triple Bottom Line Theory.
9) Discuss about the Porter and Kramer's Shared Value Theory.
10) Explain in detail about the ISO 26000.
11) Discuss about the Corporate Citizenship Model.
12) Explain in detail about the Ethical Theories of CSR.
13) Discuss about the Institutional Theories of CSR.

Q.2. Write Short Notes on:

1) Concept of CSR.
2) Evolution of CSR.
2) CSR towards Stakeholder.
4) CSR Policy.
5) CSR Governance.
6) Caroll's CSR Pyramids.
7) Stakeholder Theory of CSR.
8) Triple Bottom Line Theory.
9) Porter and Kramer's Shared Value Theory.
10) ISO 26000.
11) Corporate Citizenship Model.
12) Ethical Theories of CSR.
13) Institutional Theories of CSR.

♦♦♦

UNIT 2

Stakeholders Management and Engagement

Introduction:

Stakeholder management and engagement are critical components of modern business strategies, encompassing a multifaceted approach aimed at identifying, prioritizing, and effectively collaborating with diverse stakeholders who have a vested interest in an organization's operations, decisions, and outcomes. This dynamic process involves ongoing communication, relationship-building, and responsiveness to stakeholders' concerns, needs, and expectations. Successful stakeholder management and engagement not only enhance an organization's reputation and social license to operate but also contribute to sustainable long-term success by aligning business practices with societal and environmental goals, fostering trust, mitigating risks, and capitalizing on opportunities for innovation and growth. It is a strategic imperative for businesses to navigate the complex web of stakeholders, including customers, employees, investors, government agencies, local communities, non-governmental organizations, suppliers, and more, as they collectively influence and are influenced by an organization's activities, performance, and societal contributions. Effective stakeholder management requires a proactive, inclusive, and ethical approach that goes beyond mere compliance, recognizing that meaningful engagement fosters shared value creation and drives positive social, environmental, and economic impacts for both organizations and their broader stakeholder ecosystems.

2.1 Introduction a System Based Approach to Developing CSR:

Corporate Social Responsibility (CSR) has evolved significantly over the decades, transcending its initial perception as a charitable gesture by businesses to become a pivotal aspect of contemporary corporate strategy. The concept of CSR encompasses a broader framework that integrates social, environmental, and economic considerations into an organization's core operations, reflecting a growing recognition of the interconnectedness between businesses and the societies and environments in which they operate. This shift towards a more comprehensive understanding of CSR necessitates a systemic approach one that views businesses as integral components of complex ecosystems, where their actions have far-reaching consequences and responsibilities

A) The Evolution of CSR: From Philanthropy to Systems Thinking:

Historically, CSR was often equated with philanthropic activities, where businesses engaged in charitable endeavors without necessarily considering their impact on the core business. However, this narrow perspective has evolved into a more sophisticated understanding of CSR that recognizes its strategic significance. This evolution can be attributed to several key factors:

1) Changing Stakeholder Expectations:

As societies became more interconnected, informed, and conscious of global issues, stakeholders ranging from consumers and investors to employees and governments began to expect more from corporations. They demanded transparency, ethical behavior, and a commitment to addressing social and environmental challenges.

2) Globalization and Interconnectedness:

The globalization of markets and supply chains revealed the interdependencies between businesses, societies, and the environment. Events in one part of the world could have far-reaching consequences for businesses across borders. This heightened awareness of global interconnectedness prompted organizations to reevaluate their CSR strategies.

3) Emerging Environmental and Social Crises:

The emergence of pressing global challenges, such as climate change, social inequality, and resource depletion, underscored the need for a more systemic approach to CSR. These crises highlighted the potential risks to businesses' long-term viability and sustainability if they continued to operate in isolation from broader societal and environmental concerns.

4) Regulatory and Reporting Frameworks:

Governments and international organizations introduced regulations and reporting frameworks (e.g., the UN Global Compact, GRI Standards) that encouraged businesses to integrate CSR into their operations and disclose their social and environmental impacts.

5) Investor and Market Pressure:

Investors and financial markets increasingly recognized the materiality of ESG (Environmental, Social, and Governance) factors in assessing investment risks and opportunities. This prompted businesses to consider CSR as a means to attract and retain investment capital.

These factors, among others, have contributed to the transformation of CSR from a philanthropic endeavor to an integral part of strategic business planning. Consequently, businesses are now challenged to adopt a system-based approach that considers the broader context in which they operate and the interconnectedness of their actions with societal and environmental systems.

B) Foundations of a System-Based CSR Approach:

A system-based CSR approach builds on several foundational principles and theories, each emphasizing the interconnectedness and interdependence of various components within a broader system. These principles provide the theoretical framework for understanding and implementing CSR as an integrated, holistic endeavor:

1) Systems Thinking:

At the core of a system-based CSR approach is systems thinking, a perspective that views organizations as elements within larger systems. Systems thinking encourage businesses to consider the multiple feedback loops, dependencies, and nonlinear relationships between different elements within the system. This perspective fosters a more comprehensive understanding of the potential consequences of corporate actions.

2) Stakeholder Theory:

Stakeholder theory posits that businesses should consider the interests of all stakeholders' individuals or groups that can affect or be affected by the organization's actions. It recognizes that stakeholders play a vital role in shaping an organization's success and that their needs and concerns should be taken into account.

3) Triple Bottom Line (TBL):

The TBL framework expands the traditional notion of profit as the sole measure of success. It introduces three dimensions—economic, social, and environmental and suggests that businesses should evaluate their performance and impact in each of these areas. This multidimensional perspective aligns with the systemic view of CSR.

4) Shared Value:

Shared value, as conceptualized by Michael E. Porter and Mark R. Kramer, emphasizes that businesses can create economic value while simultaneously addressing social and environmental challenges. It recognizes that societal needs and business interests are not in conflict but can be mutually reinforcing.

5) Complexity Theory:

Complexity theory acknowledges that systems, including businesses and societies, are complex and adaptive. It highlights the inherent uncertainty and unpredictability of complex systems, suggesting that businesses must be agile and responsive in their CSR approaches.

6) **Sustainable Development Goals (SDGs):**
The United Nations' SDGs provide a globally recognized framework for addressing critical social and environmental challenges. They underscore the interconnected nature of these challenges and encourage businesses to align their CSR efforts with these broader global goals.

By drawing from these foundational principles, businesses can develop a system-based approach to CSR that goes beyond superficial, isolated initiatives and fosters a deeper understanding of the intricate web of relationships and dynamics that shape their impact on society and the environment. This approach also positions CSR as a strategic imperative that is essential for long-term resilience and competitiveness.

C) **Practical Implications of a System-Based CSR Approach:**
Implementing a system-based CSR approach involves a fundamental shift in how businesses conceptualize, plan, and execute their CSR initiatives. Here are some practical implications of this approach:

1) **Stakeholder Engagement and Collaboration:**
Businesses must engage with stakeholders at all levels of their operations. This involves active listening, dialogue, and collaboration to understand stakeholders' concerns and aspirations. Engaging stakeholders in co-creating solutions can lead to more effective and sustainable outcomes.

2) **Materiality Assessment:**
Conducting materiality assessments helps businesses identify the most significant social, environmental, and governance issues that intersect with their operations and stakeholder interests. This informs the prioritization of CSR efforts and resource allocation.

3) **Integration into Business Strategy:**
CSR should be seamlessly integrated into the core business strategy, rather than treated as a standalone function. This requires aligning CSR goals with business objectives and identifying opportunities to create shared value.

4) **Measurement and Reporting:**
Robust measurement and reporting mechanisms are essential for tracking progress and demonstrating the impact of CSR efforts. Businesses should adopt comprehensive metrics that go beyond financial indicators to capture social and environmental outcomes.

5) **Risk Assessment and Mitigation:**
System-based CSR involves anticipating and mitigating systemic risks that could impact the organization. This requires scenario planning and a proactive approach to addressing emerging challenges, such as climate change and social unrest.

6) **Innovation and R&D:**

Businesses should leverage CSR as a driver of innovation. By exploring new technologies, business models, and products that contribute to sustainability, they can gain a competitive edge while addressing societal and environmental issues.

7) **Supply Chain Responsibility:**

Given the global nature of supply chains, businesses must extend their CSR efforts to suppliers and partners. This includes promoting responsible sourcing, ethical labor practices, and sustainable production processes.

8) **Advocacy and Public Policy Engagement:**

Engaging with governments and advocating for policies that promote sustainability and responsible business practices is a critical component of a system-based CSR approach. Businesses can use their influence to shape regulatory frameworks that align with their CSR goals.

9) **Long-Term Thinking:**

A system-based CSR approach encourages businesses to adopt a long-term perspective. This includes considering the intergenerational impacts of decisions and investments in sustainable practices that endure beyond short-term financial cycles.

10) **Transparency and Accountability:**

Transparency is essential for building trust with stakeholders. Businesses should be open about their CSR efforts, disclose relevant information, and be accountable for their actions and outcomes.

D) **Transformative Potential of a System-Based CSR Approach:**

A system-based CSR approach has the potential to drive transformative change on multiple fronts:

1) **Sustainability and Resilience:**

By considering the systemic impacts of their actions, businesses can contribute to global sustainability goals and enhance their own resilience. This involves reducing negative environmental footprints, promoting social equity, and embracing responsible governance practices.

2) **Innovation and Competitive Advantage:**

A holistic CSR approach encourages businesses to innovate and develop products and services that address societal and environmental needs. This innovation can lead to new revenue streams and a competitive advantage in emerging markets.

3) **Enhanced Reputation and Brand Value:**

Businesses that demonstrate a commitment to CSR and sustainability often enjoy enhanced reputations and brand value. Consumers are increasingly making purchasing decisions based on ethical and sustainable considerations.

4) **Attracting and Retaining Talent:**

CSR initiatives that align with societal values can attract top talent and improve employee retention. Employees are more likely to be engaged and committed when they believe in their organization's purpose and impact.

5) **Managing Systemic Risks:**

A system-based approach enables businesses to better identify, assess, and manage systemic risks, such as those associated with climate change, social unrest, or supply chain disruptions.

6) **Regulatory Compliance:**

Proactive engagement with CSR can position businesses to adapt to evolving regulatory landscapes. This reduces the risk of non-compliance and associated legal and reputational consequences.

7) **Social License to Operate:**

Demonstrating a commitment to CSR and sustainability is essential for securing and maintaining the social license to operate. This is particularly important in industries with high environmental and social impacts.

8) **Global Collaboration:**

A systemic perspective encourages businesses to collaborate with other stakeholders, including governments, NGOs, and civil society, to address complex global challenges collectively.

2.2 Assessing the Current State of Company's CSR Activities:

Assessing a company's Corporate Social Responsibility (CSR) activities involves a multifaceted analysis encompassing various dimensions such as strategy, impact, stakeholder engagement, compliance, and future direction. This comprehensive evaluation is pivotal in understanding the company's commitment to sustainable and ethical practices. In exploring the current state of a company's CSR activities, several key components warrant examination, delineated below in detail.

A) **CSR Strategies:**

Effective CSR strategies lay the foundation for a company's commitment to sustainability and social responsibility. In this section, we will examine Corporation's CSR strategies.

1) **Vision and Mission Statements:**

Corporation's vision and mission statements are analyzed to identify the integration of CSR principles. These statements often provide insights into the company's overarching commitment to social and environmental responsibility.

2) **Stakeholder Engagement:**

Assessing how Corporation engages with its stakeholders, including employees, customers, suppliers, and communities, is crucial. This involves examining mechanisms for gathering feedback and incorporating stakeholder perspectives into CSR decisions.

3) Integration into Business Operations:

To what extent CSR is integrated into the company's daily operations and decision-making processes will be evaluated. This includes assessing whether CSR considerations are incorporated into supply chain management, product development, and marketing.

B) CSR Initiatives:

This section delves into specific CSR initiatives undertaken by Corporation. It examines the breadth and depth of these initiatives and their alignment with the company's CSR strategies.

1) Environmental Sustainability:

Corporation's efforts to reduce its environmental footprint will be assessed. This includes initiatives related to energy efficiency, waste reduction, water conservation, and carbon emissions reduction:

2) Social Initiatives:

The company's commitment to addressing social issues, such as diversity and inclusion, labor practices, and community development, will be analyzed. This section will also evaluate philanthropic contributions and employee volunteering programmes.

3) Ethical Business Practices:

Corporation's adherence to ethical business practices, including transparency, anti-corruption measures, and responsible sourcing, will be examined to ensure alignment with CSR principles.

C) Impact Assessment:

Assessing the impact of CSR activities is vital to determine their effectiveness in creating positive social and environmental change.

1) Key Performance Indicators (KPIs):

Corporations use of KPIs to measure the impact of its CSR initiatives will be evaluated. These may include metrics related to emissions reduction, community development, and employee satisfaction.

2) Stakeholder Feedback:

Gathering feedback from stakeholders, such as surveys and focus groups, will provide insights into the perceived impact of CSR activities. This section will analyze the company's mechanisms for receiving and responding to stakeholder feedback.

3) Case Studies and Success Stories:

Examining specific case studies and success stories related to Corporation's CSR initiatives will illustrate the tangible benefits created for society, the environment, and the company itself.

D) Performance Metrics:

Quantifiable metrics are instrumental in gauging the impact and effectiveness of CSR initiatives. This involves:

1) Environmental Impact:

Evaluate metrics related to energy consumption, waste reduction, greenhouse gas emissions, and any sustainability certifications (e.g., LEED certification).

2) Social Impact:

Analyze metrics concerning community engagement, employee volunteerism, philanthropic contributions, and social programmes' reach and effectiveness.

E) Stakeholder Engagement:

Understanding the perception and satisfaction levels of stakeholders regarding the company's CSR activities is crucial. This includes:

1) Employee Engagement:

Assess employee satisfaction, involvement in CSR activities, diversity, equity, and inclusion (DEI) initiatives, and employee feedback mechanisms.

2) Customer Perception:

Analyze customer surveys, feedback, and loyalty programmes reflecting their perception of the company's social responsibility efforts.

3) Community Relations:

Evaluate partnerships, collaborations, and initiatives aimed at benefitting local communities.

F) Transparency and Reporting:

Transparency in reporting reflects the company's commitment to accountability and open communication. This involves:

1) CSR Reports:

Review annual sustainability reports, disclosures, and public statements outlining CSR initiatives, goals, progress, and challenges.

2) Disclosure Practices:

Analyze the extent of information shared, including methodologies, performance data, and future strategies.

G) Compliance and Ethics:

Evaluate the company's commitment to ethical practices and compliance with regulations and standards:

1) **Regulatory Compliance**:

   Ensure adherence to relevant laws and regulations concerning CSR in various regions of operation.

2) **Ethical Standards**:

   Assess the company's commitment to ethical sourcing, fair labor practices, and human rights.

H) **Comparative Analysis:**

   Benchmarking the company's CSR efforts against industry peers or global standards offers valuable insights:

1) **Industry Comparisons**:

   Compare CSR practices, impact metrics, and strategies with competitors or industry leaders to identify strengths and areas for improvement.

2) **Global Standards**:

   Evaluate alignment with globally recognized CSR frameworks like the UN Sustainable Development Goals (SDGs) or Global Reporting Initiative (GRI) standards.

I) **Future Roadmap:**

   Assess the company's plans for advancing CSR initiatives:

1) **Long-term Sustainability**:

   Analyze the company's commitment to sustainable CSR practices and its integration into long-term business strategies.

2) **Innovation and Adaptation**:

   Explore how the company plans to innovate and adapt its CSR initiatives to address emerging social and environmental challenges.

2.3 Implementing CSR Programmes:

Corporate Social Responsibility (CSR) has gained prominence in recent years as businesses recognize their role in addressing societal and environmental challenges. Implementing effective CSR programmes is crucial for organizations looking to make a positive impact while maintaining ethical and sustainable business practices. This comprehensive guide explores the key steps and strategies for successfully implementing CSR programmes, offering insights, best practices, and case studies to illustrate successful approaches.

A) **Strategies for Implementing CSR Programmes:**

   Implementing Corporate Social Responsibility (CSR) programmes involves a structured approach and a commitment to balancing social, environmental, and economic considerations. Here are some strategies for effectively implementing CSR programmes:

1) **Define Clear Objectives and Goals:**
   Clearly outline the social or environmental issues your company aims to tackle through CSR initiatives. Whether it's reducing carbon footprint, supporting education, or improving community welfare, set specific, measurable, achievable, relevant, and time-bound (SMART) goals. This clarity helps direct efforts and allows for better measurement of progress and impact.
2) **Engage Stakeholders:**
   Involving diverse stakeholders - employees, customers, suppliers, and local communities is crucial. Understanding their perspectives on societal needs and incorporating their input into CSR strategies fosters inclusive, community-centered initiatives that resonate with those directly affected.
3) **Integrate CSR into Business Operations:**
   Align CSR initiatives with your company's core values and objectives. Integrate these considerations into daily operations, policies, and decision-making processes. This integration ensures that CSR isn't treated as a separate entity but becomes intrinsic to the business's ethos.
4) **Allocate Resources:**
   Commit dedicated budgets, personnel, and resources for CSR initiatives. Considering partnerships or collaborations with NGOs, governments, or other businesses can maximize impact and resource efficiency.
5) **Transparency and Reporting:**
   Maintain transparency by regularly reporting on CSR efforts. Use key performance indicators (KPIs) to measure impact. Transparent reporting builds credibility and trust among stakeholders, showcasing commitment and progress.
6) **Employee Involvement and Training:**
   Engage employees through volunteer programmes or skill-based initiatives aligned with CSR goals. Providing training enhances awareness and understanding of CSR initiatives, fostering a more engaged workforce.
7) **Innovation and Continuous Improvement:**
   Encourage innovation to address social and environmental challenges creatively. Continuous assessment and improvement based on feedback and changing circumstances ensure that CSR strategies remain effective and adaptable.
8) **Adopt Sustainable Practices:**
   Implement eco-friendly policies to reduce environmental impact. Practices like sustainable sourcing, waste reduction, and energy efficiency contribute significantly to CSR objectives.
9) **Community Engagement:**
   Support local communities through philanthropic activities, community development projects, or education initiatives. Engaging with communities directly impacted by CSR initiatives fosters trust and long-term relationships.

10) **Risk Management and Compliance:**
Identify potential risks associated with CSR initiatives and manage them effectively. Compliance with local regulations and international standards is crucial to ensuring responsible and sustainable operations.

11) **Long-term Commitment and Adaptability:**
Embrace a long-term commitment to CSR rather than viewing it as a short-term trend. Being adaptable to evolving societal needs and global challenges ensures continued relevance and impact.

12) **Communicate and Celebrate Achievements:**
Share success stories internally and externally to build credibility and inspire others. Celebrating milestones demonstrates commitment and encourages wider participation in CSR efforts.

B) Importance of Implementing CSR Programmes:
Implementing Corporate Social Responsibility (CSR) programmes holds significant importance for several reasons:

1) **Enhanced Reputation and Brand Image:**
CSR initiatives help build a positive public perception. Companies demonstrating social and environmental responsibility often enjoy better brand image and reputation, attracting customers and stakeholders who align with these values.

2) **Stakeholder Engagement and Trust:**
Engaging stakeholders through CSR programmes fosters trust and stronger relationships. Employees, customers, investors, and communities appreciate companies that contribute positively to society, leading to greater loyalty and support.

3) **Competitive Advantage:**
CSR can be a differentiator in a competitive market. Companies with robust CSR programmes can attract and retain talent, appeal to socially conscious consumers, and stand out in crowded markets.

4) **Risk Management and Longevity:**
Proactive CSR initiatives can mitigate risks associated with social or environmental issues. Addressing these concerns early helps companies avoid potential legal, financial, or reputational risks, contributing to long-term sustainability.

5) **Cost Savings and Efficiency:**
Implementing sustainable practices through CSR often leads to cost savings in the long run. Energy efficiency, waste reduction, and streamlined processes can cut operational costs while benefiting the environment.

6) **Innovation and Growth Opportunities:**
CSR programmes encourage innovation. They can spur the development of new products or services that address societal needs, opening up new markets and business opportunities.

7) **Employee Satisfaction and Retention:**
Engaging employees in meaningful CSR initiatives can improve morale, job satisfaction, and retention rates. Employees often feel proud and motivated working for companies that prioritize social responsibility.

8) **Social Impact and Contribution:**
CSR programmes create a positive impact on communities and the environment. Whether through philanthropy, community development, or environmental stewardship, companies can contribute positively to societal well-being.

9) **Regulatory Compliance and License to Operate:**
Compliance with CSR standards and regulations is increasingly becoming a requirement. Adhering to these standards ensures companies maintain their license to operate and avoid potential legal issues.

10) **Investor and Financial Benefits:**
Investors are increasingly considering a company's CSR practices in their investment decisions. Companies with strong CSR commitments may attract socially responsible investors and enjoy better access to capital.

11) **Global Relevance and Partnerships:**
In an interconnected world, CSR programmes allow companies to address global challenges and form partnerships with NGOs, governments, and other businesses to tackle complex issues collectively.

12) **Ethical Responsibility:**
Beyond business gains, implementing CSR programmes aligns with the ethical responsibility of corporations to contribute positively to society. It reflects a commitment to doing business ethically and responsibly.

2.4 Monitoring and Measuring of Impact of CSR Programmes:

Corporate Social Responsibility (CSR) has become an integral part of business operations for organizations worldwide. CSR programmes are designed to contribute positively to society, the environment, and stakeholders while also aligning with the organization's values and objectives. To ensure that CSR initiatives are effective and provide the intended benefits, it is essential to monitor and measure their impact comprehensively. This article explores the importance of monitoring and measuring the impact of CSR programmes, the key steps involved, and various tools and frameworks available for this purpose. Corporate Social Responsibility (CSR) is a strategic approach where businesses voluntarily integrate social and environmental concerns into their operations and interactions with stakeholders. CSR programmes encompass a wide range of initiatives, including philanthropy, sustainability efforts, ethical business practices, and community engagement. These initiatives aim to create positive impacts on various stakeholders like employees, customers, communities & the environment.

A) Key Steps in Monitoring and Measuring Impact of CSR Programmes:

Monitoring and measuring the impact of Corporate Social Responsibility (CSR) programmes is essential to assess their effectiveness and demonstrate accountability. To achieve meaningful results, organizations should follow a structured approach. Here are the key steps in monitoring and measuring CSR impact:

1) Define Clear Objectives:

Start by defining specific, measurable, and time-bound objectives for your CSR programmes. These objectives should align with your organization's mission, values, and strategic goals.

2) Identify Key Performance Indicators (KPIs):

Determine the KPIs that will help you measure progress toward your CSR objectives. These indicators should be quantifiable and relevant to your initiatives. Common KPIs include carbon emissions reduction, community engagement metrics, employee volunteer hours, and charitable contributions.

3) Baseline Assessment:

Before implementing CSR initiatives, establish a baseline measurement of the current state of affairs related to your chosen KPIs. This baseline will serve as a reference point for future comparisons.

4) Data Collection:

Collect relevant data from various sources, including internal records, surveys, interviews, and external research. Ensure that the data collected is accurate, reliable, and consistent.

5) Data Analysis:

Analyze the collected data to evaluate the impact of your CSR programmes. This involves comparing current performance against the baseline data and assessing progress toward your objectives.

Use statistical analysis and data visualization tools to identify trends, correlations, and areas for improvement.

6) Stakeholder Engagement and Feedback:

Engage with stakeholders, including employees, customers, suppliers, and community members, to gather qualitative feedback on the impact of CSR initiatives. Stakeholder input can provide valuable insights and help measure intangible impacts like reputation and social capital.

7) Financial Assessment:

Conduct a financial analysis to assess the costs and benefits of your CSR programmes. Calculate the return on investment (ROI) by comparing the financial outlays with the economic and social returns generated by these initiatives.

8) **Reporting and Communication**:

Develop comprehensive CSR impact reports that communicate the results of your monitoring and measurement efforts. These reports should be tailored to different stakeholder groups and should be clear, transparent, and accessible. Regularly communicate your CSR achievements, progress, and areas for improvement to internal and external stakeholders through various channels, including annual reports, websites, and social media.

9) **Review and Adapt**:

Continuously review the results of your monitoring and measurement efforts. Use this information to adapt and refine your CSR programmes as necessary. Consider revising objectives, changing strategies, or reallocating resources to maximize impact.

10) **Benchmarking**:

Compare your CSR performance with industry peers or best practices to gain insights into how your organization stacks up. Benchmarking can identify areas where you excel and areas where you may need to improve.

B) Tools and Frameworks for Monitoring and Measuring Impact of CSR Programmes:

Monitoring and measuring the impact of Corporate Social Responsibility (CSR) programmes requires the use of appropriate tools and frameworks to gather and analyze data effectively. Here are some commonly used tools and frameworks for monitoring and measuring CSR impact:

1) **Global Reporting Initiative (GRI):**

The GRI provides a comprehensive set of sustainability reporting guidelines and standards. Organizations can use the GRI framework to report on their economic, environmental, and social performance. GRI standards offer a structured approach to measuring and disclosing CSR impacts and align with global reporting best practices.

2) **Social Return on Investment (SROI):**

SROI is a methodology for quantifying the social and environmental value created by CSR initiatives. It assigns monetary values to the non-financial impacts of projects, making it easier to compare the social and financial returns on investment. SROI analysis can help organizations assess the effectiveness and efficiency of their CSR efforts.

3) **ISO 26000:**

ISO 26000 is an international standard that provides guidance on social responsibility. It offers a framework for integrating CSR into an organization's strategy and operations. While not a certification standard, ISO 26000 can be used as a reference for measuring the social & environmental impacts of CSR activities.

4) **Sustainability Reporting Standards (SASB):**
SASB offers industry-specific sustainability accounting standards that help organizations identify and report on material ESG (Environmental, Social, and Governance) issues relevant to their industry. These standards provide a consistent framework for measuring CSR impact and align with financial reporting.

5) **The United Nations Sustainable Development Goals (SDGs):**
The UN SDGs are a set of 17 global goals that address various social and environmental challenges. Organizations can use the SDGs as a framework to align their CSR initiatives with international sustainability objectives. Tracking progress toward specific SDGs can be an effective way to measure impact.

6) **Benefit-Cost Analysis (BCA):**
BCA is a quantitative method used to assess the economic and social costs and benefits of CSR programmes. It involves comparing the total costs of an initiative with its anticipated benefits, both in monetary and non-monetary terms. BCA can help organizations determine the financial viability and overall impact of their CSR projects.

7) **Key Performance Indicators (KPIs):**
Developing and tracking specific KPIs that align with CSR objectives is a common approach to measurement. These KPIs should be tailored to the organization's goals and may include metrics related to environmental sustainability, employee engagement, community involvement, and customer satisfaction.

8) **Stakeholder Surveys and Feedback Mechanisms:**
Collecting feedback from stakeholders through surveys, interviews, and focus groups can provide qualitative insights into the impact of CSR programmes. This qualitative data complements quantitative metrics and helps organizations understand stakeholder perceptions and expectations.

9) **Third-Party Auditing and Certification:**
Organizations can engage third-party auditors or certification bodies to independently assess and validate the impact of their CSR programmes. Third-party verification enhances credibility and transparency, especially when seeking external recognition or certification, such as B Corp certification.

10) **CSR Software and Reporting Platforms:**
There are various software tools and platforms designed specifically for CSR reporting and data management. Examples include CSRware, Enablon, and Sales force Impact Cloud. These tools streamline data collection, analysis, and reporting processes.

11) **Customized Impact Assessment Models:**
Some organizations develop customized impact assessment models tailored to their specific CSR initiatives. These models can include financial models, social impact

models, and environmental impact models, allowing organizations to measure the multifaceted impact of their programmes.

C) Importance of Monitoring and Measuring Impact of CSR Programmes:

Monitoring and measuring the impact of CSR programmes are crucial for several key reasons:

1) Accountability and Transparency:

CSR initiatives are often communicated to stakeholders, including investors, customers, employees, and the public, as part of an organization's commitment to social responsibility. Monitoring and measuring CSR impact provide tangible evidence that the organization is fulfilling its promises. This fosters trust and demonstrates accountability, which is essential for maintaining a positive reputation.

2) Strategic Decision-Making:

Monitoring and measuring CSR impact generate data and insights that organizations can use for strategic decision-making. By understanding the effectiveness of various initiatives, companies can allocate resources more efficiently, prioritize high-impact projects, and refine their CSR strategy over time.

3) Continuous Improvement:

Regularly assessing CSR impact allows organizations to identify areas where they can improve. This iterative process ensures that CSR initiatives remain relevant and effective in addressing social and environmental challenges. It also helps companies adapt to changing circumstances and stakeholder expectations.

4) Risk Mitigation:

CSR initiatives can carry risks, such as unintended negative consequences or backlash if they are perceived as insincere or ineffective. Monitoring allows organizations to identify and address these risks early, reducing the likelihood of reputational damage or legal issues.

5) Alignment with Objectives:

Many organizations engage in CSR to align with their core values and mission. Measuring the impact ensures that CSR initiatives are congruent with these objectives. If there is a misalignment, organizations can adjust their programmes to better reflect their values and purpose.

6) Stakeholder Engagement:

Engaging with stakeholders is a fundamental aspect of CSR. Monitoring and measuring CSR impact provide opportunities to interact with stakeholders, seek their feedback, and incorporate their perspectives into program improvement. This engagement can lead to stronger relationships with stakeholders who value an organization's commitment to CSR.

7) Competitive Advantage:

Organizations that can demonstrate positive CSR impacts may gain a competitive advantage. Consumers are increasingly making purchasing decisions based on a company's social and environmental performance. Investors also consider CSR performance as an indicator of long-term sustainability and profitability.

8) Regulatory Compliance:

In some jurisdictions, there are legal requirements or reporting obligations related to CSR activities. Monitoring and measuring CSR impact help ensure compliance with these regulations and reduce the risk of non-compliance penalties.

9) Employee Engagement and Retention:

Employees often seek purpose and meaning in their work. Being part of an organization that contributes positively to society and the environment can boost employee morale, engagement, and retention. Regularly communicating the impact of CSR initiatives reinforces employees' sense of pride and purpose.

10) Long-Term Sustainability:

CSR is not just a short-term marketing tactic. It is a commitment to making a positive and sustainable impact over the long term. Monitoring and measuring help organizations assess the long-term effects of their actions and make necessary adjustments to ensure sustainability.

D) Challenges and Considerations in Monitoring and Measuring Impact of CSR Programmes:

Here are some of the key challenges and considerations in monitoring and measuring Impact of CSR programmes:

1) Data Collection and Quality:

Gathering accurate and reliable data can be challenging, especially when dealing with qualitative and intangible impacts such as social capital or employee morale. Ensuring data quality and consistency across different sources and time periods is essential.

2) Baseline Establishment:

Setting a meaningful baseline for comparison is crucial, but it can be difficult, particularly for organizations that are new to CSR measurement. Determining what data to collect before starting a program can be a challenge.

3) Defining Appropriate Metrics:

Selecting the right Key Performance Indicators (KPIs) and metrics is essential. However, it can be challenging to identify metrics that accurately reflect the intended social, environmental, and economic impacts of CSR initiatives.

4) Complexity of Impact:

CSR initiatives often have multifaceted impacts that extend beyond immediate outcomes. These complexities can make it challenging to capture the full range of consequences and dependencies associated with CSR programmes.

5) **Attribution and Causality:**
Establishing a direct causal link between CSR initiatives and their impacts can be challenging. Many factors can influence outcomes, making it difficult to attribute changes solely to CSR efforts.

6) **Timeframes and Lag Effects:**
Some CSR impacts, particularly those related to social and behavioral change, may take time to manifest. Lag effects can make it challenging to assess the immediate success of initiatives.

7) **Scope and Scale:**
Organizations with a global presence or multiple CSR initiatives may find it challenging to standardize measurement across diverse projects, regions, or business units.

8) **Resource Constraints:**
Dedicated resources, both financial and human, are required for effective monitoring and measurement. Smaller organizations or those with limited budgets may struggle to allocate resources to this task.

9) **Qualitative Aspects:**
Not all CSR impacts can be quantified easily. Qualitative aspects, such as stakeholder perceptions, cultural changes, or community relationships, are crucial but may require more subjective evaluation.

10) **Stakeholder Engagement:**
Engaging with stakeholders to gather their perspectives can be time-consuming and may involve challenges in reaching diverse stakeholder groups, managing expectations, and interpreting qualitative feedback.

11) **Benchmarking and Standards:**
The absence of universally accepted benchmarks and standards for CSR measurement can make it challenging to compare performance across organizations or industries. Companies may need to develop their own measurement frameworks.

12) **Data Privacy and Security:**
Collecting and storing data related to CSR impact must adhere to data privacy and security regulations. Organizations need to ensure that data is handled in a compliant and ethical manner.

2.5 Moral and Economic Arguments for CSR:

Corporate Social Responsibility (CSR) is a concept that has evolved over time, transitioning from a philanthropic add-on to an integral part of modern business practices. It encompasses a company's commitment to balancing profit generation with positive contributions to society and the environment. This essay aims to provide a comprehensive analysis of CSR, focusing on its moral underpinnings and economic justifications.

A) Moral Arguments for CSR:

Corporate Social Responsibility (CSR) is often supported by a range of moral and ethical arguments. These arguments emphasize the responsibilities and ethical obligations that businesses have toward society and various stakeholders. Here are some key moral arguments for CSR:

1) Stakeholder Theory:

This theory argues that businesses have ethical responsibilities not only to their shareholders but to all stakeholders, including employees, customers, suppliers, communities, and the environment. Embracing CSR is seen as a way to balance and fulfill these obligations.

2) Ethical Duty:

Some proponents of CSR argue that businesses, as entities that benefit from society, have a moral duty to give back and contribute positively to society. This duty is often framed in terms of reciprocity; businesses should contribute to the well-being of the society that supports them.

3) Sustainable Development:

CSR is seen as a way to promote sustainable development, which aligns with moral principles of intergenerational equity. This argument emphasizes the responsibility of businesses to ensure that their actions do not harm future generations' ability to meet their needs.

4) Environmental Ethics:

Environmental ethics underline the moral obligation of businesses to protect and preserve the environment. CSR initiatives that focus on sustainability, reducing pollution, and conserving resources are seen as ethically responsible actions.

5) Social Justice:

CSR can contribute to social justice by addressing issues of inequality, poverty, and social exclusion. Businesses can use their resources and influence to support marginalized communities and promote a fairer society.

6) Human Rights:

Businesses have a responsibility to respect and uphold human rights, both within their operations and throughout their supply chains. This includes ensuring fair labor practices and avoiding complicity in human rights abuses.

7) Ethical Consumption:

As consumers increasingly seek ethically produced and sustainable products, businesses have a moral obligation to meet these demands by adopting CSR practices that align with consumer values.

8) **Ethical Leadership:**

Businesses are often seen as leaders in society. Embracing CSR can set a positive example and encourage other organizations to follow suit, contributing to broader positive social change.

9) **Trust and Reputation:**

Ethical behavior and CSR initiatives can enhance a company's reputation and build trust among customers, employees, and investors. Ethical companies are more likely to be seen as trustworthy and reliable.

10) **Avoiding Harm:**

One fundamental moral argument for CSR is the avoidance of harm. Businesses should take proactive measures to prevent harm to people, communities, and the environment caused by their operations.

11) **Long-Term Success:**

Ethical behavior and CSR are often linked to long-term business success. Companies that prioritize ethical conduct are more likely to enjoy sustained profitability and avoid reputational damage.

12) **Cultural and Ethical Values:**

Businesses often operate within societies that have specific cultural and ethical values. Adhering to these values is seen as a moral duty, and CSR initiatives that align with local values are considered ethically responsible.

B) **Economic Arguments for CSR:**

Corporate Social Responsibility (CSR) is often associated with economic benefits for businesses, as well as for society at large. While CSR initiatives may involve upfront costs, there are several economic arguments that demonstrate how CSR can ultimately contribute to a company's financial success. Here are some key economic arguments for CSR:

1) **Enhanced Reputation and Brand Image:**

A positive CSR reputation can enhance a company's brand image and reputation in the eyes of consumers. This can lead to increased customer loyalty, higher sales, and the ability to charge premium prices for products or services.

2) **Customer Attraction and Retention:**

Many consumers prefer to do business with socially responsible companies. CSR initiatives can attract new customers who share the same values and help retain existing customers, which can boost sales and profitability.

3) **Risk Mitigation:**

CSR practices can help mitigate various risks, including legal and regulatory risks, reputational risks, and supply chain risks. Addressing environmental and social issues proactively can prevent costly legal disputes and damage to a company's reputation.

4) **Cost Reduction:**
CSR initiatives that focus on resource efficiency, waste reduction, and sustainable practices can lead to cost savings in the long run. For example, energy-efficient operations can reduce utility bills, and waste reduction can cut disposal costs.

5) **Employee Engagement and Productivity:**
A strong CSR program can improve employee morale and engagement. Engaged employees tend to be more productive, which can positively impact a company's bottom line through increased efficiency and innovation.

6) **Access to Capital:**
Some investors, particularly socially responsible investment (SRI) funds and impact investors prefer to invest in companies with strong CSR performance. Access to capital may be easier and more affordable for businesses with a positive CSR track record.

7) **Competitive Advantage:**
CSR initiatives can provide a competitive advantage in the marketplace. Companies that demonstrate ethical and sustainable practices can differentiate themselves from competitors and gain a larger market share.

8) **Innovation and Adaptation:**
CSR can drive innovation by encouraging companies to develop new products and technologies that meet sustainability and societal needs. This innovation can lead to new revenue streams and business opportunities.

9) **Long-Term Sustainability:**
Sustainable business practices, including responsible resource management and ethical supply chain management, contribute to the long-term sustainability of a company's operations. This stability can enhance financial resilience.

10) **Access to New Markets:**
CSR initiatives can open doors to new markets and business opportunities. Some governments and organizations prefer to partner with socially responsible companies for procurement and business collaborations.

11) **Customer Feedback and Product Improvement:**
Engaging in CSR can provide valuable customer feedback, which can inform product or service improvements. Meeting customer expectations can lead to increased sales and market share.

12) **Talent Attraction and Retention:**
A strong commitment to CSR can attract top talent and reduce employee turnover. Recruiting and retaining skilled employees can lead to productivity gains and cost savings associated with recruitment and training.

♦♦♦

Multiple Choice Questions

1) **Introducing a systems-based approach to developing CSR involves considering the ------------ impact of business operations.**
   a) Sole b) Holistic c) Narrow d) Random
2) **Assessing the current state of a company's CSR activities requires a thorough ------------ of existing initiatives.**
   a) Analysis b) Neglect c) Acceptance d) Disregard
3) **Implementing CSR programs necessitates the integration of ethical values into ------------ strategies.**
   a) Profit-maximizing b) Isolation
   c) Expansionist d) Business
4) **Monitoring and measuring the impact of CSR programs involves establishing ------------ indicators.**
   a) Vague b) Ambiguous c) Measurable d) Intangible
5) **Moral and economic arguments for CSR emphasize the alignment of business practices with ------------ values.**
   a) Ethical b) Arbitrary c) Exploitative d) Ambiguous
6) **A systems-based approach to developing CSR recognizes the interconnectedness of social, ------------, and environmental factors.**
   a) Cultural b) Sole c) Narrow d) Economic
7) **In assessing the current state of a company's CSR activities, a comprehensive ------------ is essential.**
   a) Excuse b) Evaluation c) Neglect d) Indifference
8) **Implementing CSR programs requires the engagement of employees and key ------------.**
   a) Stakeholders b) Competitors c) Isolators d) Observers
9) **Monitoring and measuring the impact of CSR programs is crucial for ensuring ------------ accountability.**
   a) Unethical b) Indisputable c) Arbitrary d) Isolated
10) **Moral arguments for CSR emphasize the ------------ obligation of businesses to contribute positively to society.**
   a) Economic b) Ethical c) Profitable d) Isolated
11) **A systems-based approach to developing CSR considers the ------------ effects of business decisions.**
   a) Singular b) Holistic c) Limited d) Negligible
12) **Assessing the current state of a company's CSR activities involves identifying areas for ------------.**

a) Preservation b) Improvement c) Neglect d) Profit

13) Implementing CSR programs requires a commitment to long-term ------------.

a) Expansion b) Sustainability c) Neglect d) Profit

14) Monitoring and measuring the impact of CSR programs allows businesses to demonstrate ------------.

a) Isolation b) Secrecy c) Accountability d) Neglect

15) Economic arguments for CSR highlight the positive impact on ----------- and long-term profitability.

a) Neglect b) Consumerism c) Stakeholders d) Ambitions

16) A systems-based approach to developing CSR recognizes the ----------- nature of social and environmental issues.

a) Narrow b) Interconnected
c) Arbitrary d) Neglectful

17) Assessing the current state of a company's CSR activities involves evaluating the alignment with ----------- values.

a) Sole b) Ethical c) Arbitrary d) Negligent

18) Implementing CSR programs requires clear ----------- and allocation of resources.

a) Ambiguity b) Vagueness c) Objectives d) Neglect

19) Monitoring and measuring the impact of CSR programs enables businesses to identify areas for ------------.

a) Ambiguity b) Improvement c) Neglect d) Expansion

20) Moral arguments for CSR stress the importance of businesses contributing to the ----------- good.

a) Narrow b) Holistic c) Arbitrary d) Neglectful

21) A systems-based approach to developing CSR involves recognizing the ----------- of various stakeholders.

a) Narrowness b) Ambiguity c) Interests d) Neglect

22) Assessing the current state of a company's CSR activities helps in identifying areas for ----------- and innovation.

a) Preservation b) Improvement c) Neglect d) Profit

23) Implementing CSR programs requires a ----------- commitment to social and environmental goals.

a) Limited b) Neglectful c) Sincere d) Ambiguous

24) Monitoring and measuring the impact of CSR programs involves using ----------- metrics.

a) Subjective b) Ambiguous c) Measurable d) Indistinct

25) Economic arguments for CSR underline the long-term benefits of ------------ business practices.

a) Ethical b) Sustainable c) Exploitative d) Arbitrary

Ans : **1)** b, **2)** b, **3)** d, **4)** c, **5)** a, **6)** d, **7)** b, **8)** a, **9)** b, **10)** b, **11)** b, **12)** b, **13)** b, **14)** c, **15)** c, **16)** b, **17)** b, **18)** c, **19)** b, **20)** b, **21)** c, **22)** b, **23)** c, **24)** c, **25)** b.

♦♦♦

Review Questions

Q.1. Answer the Following Questions:

1) Explain in detail about the System Based Approach to Developing CSR.
2) Discuss about the Assessing a Current State of Company's CSR Activities.
3) Explain the Strategies for Implementing CSR Programmes.
4) State the Importance of Implementing CSR Programmes.
5) Explain the Monitoring and Measuring Impact of CSR Programmes.
6) Discuss about the Moral Arguments for CSR.
7) Explain the Economic Argument for CSR.

Q.2. Write Short Notes on:

1) System Based Approach to Developing CSR
2) Assessing a Current State of Company's CSR Activities.
3) Implementing CSR Programmes.
4) Monitoring and Measuring Impact of CSR Programmes.
5) Moral Argument for CSR.
6) Economic Argument for CSR.

♦♦♦

NOTES